the
org

the easy organizer

365 TIPS FOR CONQUERING CLUTTER

Marilyn Bohn

BETTERWAY HOME
CINCINNATI, OHIO
WWW.BETTERWAYBOOKS.COM

Contents

Introduction

You are holding in your hands a valuable organizing resource book that can help you with all of your basic organizing needs. This book is filled with tips and ideas on how to organize almost everything in your home.

You don't need to read this book through cover to cover before you get started with your organizing projects, but I highly recommend you read chapter one, "Key Organizing Concepts," before you start.

After you are familiar with the key organizing concepts, identify what you want to organize in your home and then jump straight to the chapter that addresses that subject.

The information in this book is the same information I share with clients as a professional organizer. One day as I was going about my daily routine, it came to me that many (if not every single one) of the women I work with ask me the same questions about organizing. I thought it would be wonderful if I answered their questions and many more by writing another book that would be laid out by room, giving tips and answering specific questions for each room or space. My hope is that you will use this book as you organize and will feel as if a professional organizer is beside you answering your questions and giving you tips and ideas to help you reach your organizing goals.

ONE

Key Organizing Concepts

- Create your organized aesthetic.
- Stop trying to be a perfectionist.
- Do like things together.
- Keep clutter out of your home.
- Separate emotions from possessions.
- Take tortoise steps.
- Use a belongs-elsewhere basket.
- Organize from the inside out.
- Keep likes with likes.
- Assign homes for everything.
- Keep things where you use them.
- Make it easy to put things away.

- Prioritize your everyday space.
- Prioritize your storage spaces.
- When you finish using something, put it away.
- Keep a donation bin handy and use it.
- Keep flat surfaces clear.
- Declutter daily.
- Tidy up every evening.
- Organize for the next day.
- Make a plan to revisit spaces.

The tips in this chapter can be applied to any organizing project. Using these concepts makes the organizing process crystal clear and will keep you organized. Think of them as your organizing cheat sheet or guide.

If you apply these concepts on a daily, weekly, or monthly basis, being organized will become a way of life. Life happens and circumstances change, so you will need to continually evaluate the organizing systems in your home.

Create your organized aesthetic.

People often think a room or area is only organized if it is clean and spartan. We associate organization with a specific look or aesthetic—typically one created by a magazine. The truth is there isn't a uniform look when it comes to organizing. It's your home; arrange it to meet your standards of beauty and comfort.

Your home is organized if you know where to find everything in it. By this standard, a very messy room could still be defined as organized if its owner knows exactly where to find everything in the room.

If you don't like a lot of structure, give yourself flexibility with your organizing. Make it as easy as possible to find things when you need them and put them away when you are finished. For example, you don't have to keep your movie collection alphabetized for it to be organized. In this situation, you may find the movies are "organized enough" when they are all kept together in the same place.

Stop trying to be a perfectionist.

We have a love-hate relationship with glossy magazine photos. They inspire us to organize our home, but they also discourage us because we know we can't reach that level of perfection. Stop comparing your home to those photos. Your home doesn't have to look like a picture in a magazine to be organized.

When you have things where you can find them without searching and you and your family are comfortable with what you have and the way it's organized, then it is good enough. It doesn't have to be perfect (or even tidy all the time) to be organized; the important thing is that it works for you.

Do like things together.

To make the most of your time, start each day by making a list of what you need to do. Then prioritize the items in the list and group like tasks together, such as making phone calls, filing, or running errands. This saves time, money, effort, and energy.

Keep clutter out of your home.

Resist buying something you don't love, won't use, or don't need. A sale is not a sale if you don't have a place for the item or it doesn't meet the first three criteria.

Stop subscribing to magazines you never read. Get your name off of junk mail lists so you don't have piles of mailers cluttering your home.

If you are a collector but no longer enjoy your collection, stop collecting and tell your family and friends you no longer want gifts related to that collection.

Separate emotions from possessions.

Many people hold on to objects because they believe the object holds the memory. If you're worried you'll forget, take a photo of the object, put it in a scrapbook, and write down your favorite memory of it. Then give the object away knowing you've transferred the memory from the object to your scrapbook.

It also can be hard to get rid of inherited items. Understand that you can't keep everything. Select your most sentimental items to keep and give the rest to family members, friends or charities who can use them. Share the story of your loved one when you pass on his or her items. Honor the items you keep by properly displaying or storing them in your home.

Take tortoise steps.

You know the story of the tortoise and the hare. The tortoise won the race against the hare even though she was the slower of the two. She just kept going slowly and surely until she finished. This is how it is with organizing. Do it a little at a time so you don't get burned out.

When starting a big project, set your timer for about twenty minutes. Give yourself permission to stop after that length of time. If you are in a good rhythm, then return to organizing, but don't do so much at one time that you become discouraged and overloaded. You will be surprised at how much you will accomplish by taking it slow.

We all seem to underestimate how long it takes to get rid of clutter. If you think a project will take an hour, plan ninety minutes to two hours so you won't be disappointed when it takes longer than you estimated.

Use a belongs-elsewhere basket.

Whenever you organize or tidy a room, keep a basket or container with you for items that belong in other rooms of the house. This keeps you in the room you're working on and let's you focus all of your energy on the task at hand. When you finish organizing, remove the basket and put the items where they belong.

Organize from the inside out.

When organizing a room, start organizing from the inside—drawers, cupboards, containers, and closets—and then organize other parts of the room, such as flat surfaces, and the open floor space. This method works for three reasons:

1. Things out in the open need a place to go.
2. You need to make room in drawers, containers and cupboards to hold things that were left in the open.
3. You'll handle each item only once. There is no sense in putting things away and then having to remove everything to organize that space.

Keep likes with likes.

Like items are simply things that have something in common. They could be identical items (such as a set of drinking glasses) or similar items (such as all of your movies). Or they could relate to each other because they serve the same purpose (such as all your supplies for a specific hobby).

Keep like items together so you only have to look in one place when you want a specific item. For example, if you keep all of your movies in a cabinet in your living room, you can go straight to the cabinet when you want a movie instead of looking in multiple locations around your home.

Have duplicates of items that you use in several places in your home. Scissors are needed in different areas, such as the office, kitchen, and craft room. In every room where you have duplicates, keep like items together.

Assign homes for everything.

How many times have you heard, "A place for everything and everything in its place?" When everything has its own specific home, you can find things quickly and easily. Objects that don't have a home become clutter because they are set down in random locations where they don't really belong.

If you don't know where a specific item belongs and it has a tendency to join other clutter, stop and think about where you would look for it when you need it; then create a permanent home for it in that location.

Keep things where you use them.

To save time and energy, organize things so they are easy to access, are visible, and are easy to put away after being used. For example: put the dish soap near the sink or dishwasher, place the plates and bowls where they are easy to reach and to put away when taking them out of the dishwasher. Store blankets and sheets near the rooms where they are used. Keep sports equipment together, in separate containers for each sport, in the same area. Keep cleaning supplies in each bathroom if there's room.

Make it easy to put things away.

It's easier to get things out than to put them away, so make it easy to put things away. Think ahead when setting up an organizing system. Consider how your family is used to doing things and incorporate their habits into any new organizing system. This is easier than trying to change them.

Prioritize your everyday space.

Save time and frustration by prioritizing the spaces in your home. Spaces can include shelves, drawers, sections of a room, or an entire room. Give each space one of the following designations:

Premium space: This is the space you use almost on a daily basis, is the easiest to reach, and is the most convenient to take things from and return things to. Keep items you use every day in premium spaces. Examples of premium spaces are: kitchen drawers and cabinets, eye-level bookcases or shelves in your living areas, bedroom closet rod, floor, and convenient shelves, vanities and medicine cabinets (if hygiene or cosmetic items are kept here).

Secondary spaces: These spaces are on higher or lower shelves, in the backs of closets and other accessible but slightly inconvenient spaces. You may need to bend or use a stepstool to reach them. Use these areas to store things that are used about once a week. They may take a little more effort to get out and return, but that's okay because they are semi convenient and aren't used every day.

Semi-storage: Items kept in semi-storage are typically used once a year such as holiday decorations, seasonal dishes, seasonal clothing and camping gear or beach supplies. Store these items where they can be accessed but aren't taking up valuable space within your home. These items can be kept in your attic or storage room, then rotated in and out of your closets and living space as needed.

Prioritize your storage spaces.

When you put something into storage, categorize it as short-term or long-term. Short-term storage items are used at least once a year. Examples are seasonal clothing and holiday decorations.

Long-term storage is for things you are storing but have to look at only every few years, if at all. These can be things you are storing for adult children who have moved away, or inherited items you are keeping to pass on to other family members in the future. Long-term storage items can go on the bottom of stacks and on high or low shelves.

When you finish using something, put it away.

Clutter attracts more clutter. A pile starts with just one item. Before you put something down, instead of putting it away, stop and ask yourself when you are going to have more time than right now to put it where it belongs.

As my friend says, "Don't put it down, put it away," and "Spend a couple of seconds putting it away now or half a day looking for it if you don't."

Keep a donation bin handy and use it.

In your garage or in a closet, keep a bag or a box labeled "donation." When you find something you don't use or don't want, immediately put it in the donation bin. When the bin is full, take it to your local thrift store or another charity.

Keep flat surfaces clear.

Flat surfaces can truly become clutter magnets. When one thing is laid down, then another thing comes along and joins it until the entire surface is covered with things that don't belong.

Make a rule in your home that nothing will be allowed on flat surfaces that doesn't belong there. Provide attractive containers to give things homes that are most often placed on flat surfaces. Back up this rule with consequences. Take the item away and have the owner pay money or do an extra job around the home to get it back, or donate it after a reasonable length of time.

Declutter daily.

When you find things out of place, immediately put them back where they belong. Don't wait for another day or time to put things back in place. Put items in your donation bin as soon as you decide you don't want them. Organizing doesn't have to be done in huge chunks of time; when it is done a little at a time, you can keep organized.

Tidy up every evening.

Take five or ten minutes every evening to tidy up every room in your home. Include your family in this task. Put away everything you got out during the day. Take all dirty dishes to the kitchen and load the dishwasher. Pick up blankets and pillows. Put away projects and toys. Empty your stairs basket and BE (belongs-else-where) basket. Doing this every day will keep clutter away.

Organize for the next day.

Prepare for the next morning every night. Organize the things you will need in the morning. Lay out clothes, check all home-work and put it in backpacks, pack lunches. Check your sched-ule to see what items you will need such as sports equipment, lunch money, or items needed for errands. Place anything you or your children will need next to the door you leave from. Check the batteries on cell phones and other electronics and charge them if needed.

Make a plan to revisit spaces.

Just because a space is organized once doesn't mean it will statically stay organized. Every few months revisit drawers, cupboards, and closets to put strays in their place and see if you want to keep everything that is there. You may find a better way to organize the same space based on the way you use it.

TWO

Time

1 Work with no interruptions.

2 Use a day planner.

3 Use schedules.

4 Create routines.

5 Use a family calendar.

6 Establish your priorities.

7 Write lists.

8 Keep a record.

9 Use a timer.

10 Schedule projects around your energy level.

11 Practice saying "no."

12 Give a thought-out response.

13 Delegate as often as possible.

14 Give up on being a perfectionist.

15 Let go of fear.

16 Make time to rest.

17 Take steps to overcome procrastination.

18 Eat the elephant one bite at a time.

19 Be intentional with your time on the phone.

20 Take control of your e-mail.

21 Limit your time on the computer.

22 Consolidate your errands.

23 Plan ahead to minimize your wait time.

24 Tailor your chauffeuring services.

25 Multitask the smart way.

26 Good mornings begin in the evening.

27 Use the right tools for the job.

28 Practice preventative maintenance.

29 Use labels whenever possible.

30 Recognize that clutter costs you time.

31 Handle items only once.

We all want to spend less time on obligations we have to do and devote more time to our passions, interests, hobbies, family and friends. There never seems to be enough time in the day to do everything.

When you organize your schedule and are intentional with your actions, you can finish tasks faster and therefore give yourself more time to do what you want to do instead of what you have to do. Follow the quick tips in this chapter to save time.

1. Work with no interruptions.

Any project—whether it's at work or at home—goes faster if you aren't interrupted or distracted by the phone, other people, or e-mail.

When you're working on a project at home, let your family know you won't be available for a certain length of time. (Then stick with your plan so they will know you are serious).

Work while children are taking naps or hire a babysitter for a few hours. Or exchange child care with a friend for a few hours a week to give each of you a break. Let your phone take messages, and return calls at your predetermined time.

In the office, turn off your e-mail notification and set your phone to do not disturb so you can focus your efforts.

2. Use a day planner.

Using a daily planner is one of the most important things you can do to organize your life. It helps you track your daily, weekly, and monthly activities so you don't have conflicting commitments, and it helps you manage your time effectively.

Choose a planner that fits your style. It can be paper or electronic, but make sure you can easily carry it with you at all times. Among other things, in your planner record:

- daily appointments
- to-do lists
- activities
- addresses and phone numbers
- gift lists
- shopping lists
- birthdays and anniversaries
- children's activities

3. Use schedules.

A set schedule helps you remember and efficiently complete routine tasks.

Create a schedule that works for your lifestyle. Write it on a calendar or in a planner—paper or electronic.

Start by scheduling things you do on a daily basis:

- wake-up time
- morning routine
- meal times
- work and school hours
- regular appointments, meetings, etc.
- exercise
- bed time

Then plan other activities around these daily activities. Be realistic about what you can accomplish in one day. When you take on more than you can handle, you set yourself up for stress and failure. If you don't accomplish something, move it to the next day if it's something you still want to do.

4. Create routines.

Routines help relieve stress. You gain peace of mind when you focus on what you want or need to do. Routines also bring order to your days. Children as well as adults like routines because they bring a sense of control and security to their lives.

Set up flexible routines for things that happen daily: Hold a family council and brainstorm what activities each family member needs to do on a daily basis. On a white board or calendar set up a schedule and then follow it. Common routines are:

- **Morning:** grooming, hygiene, and chores needed to start the day plus breakfast
- **After school/work:** unloading bags, completing chores and homework
- **Dinner:** cooking, setting the table, and clean up
- **Bedtime:** grooming and hygiene plus prep for the next day (e.g., laying out clothes or filling a backpack) and a quick tidy up around the house

You also may need to establish a few different routines that are used on specific days of the week or tied to regularly occurring activities, such as a rehearsal, meeting, or event.

5. Use a family calendar.

For busy families, a main reference calendar that shows each family member's schedule is a must.

A large wall calendar with squares large enough to write several activities per day works well. Hang the calendar in a location that everyone will see daily, such as the kitchen wall.

To make the calendar quick and easy to read, assign each family member his or her own pen color so you can tell at a glance where each person needs to be. Also include a specific color to indicate events the entire family will attend together. Give this a try and, if you find it too confusing or too time-consuming to maintain, use just one color. Don't give up on the calendar. Figure out how to make it work for you and your family.

At least once a week, or as new activities are added, compare your personal calendar with the family calendar to ensure events aren't left out or double-booked.

6. Establish your priorities.

Setting realistic priorities can help you get organized. Prioritizing can also give you a sense of freedom by letting you know what you have to do and then setting a specific order to accomplish your desired results.

Prioritize by setting up a system such as:

Highest priority: These are activities you absolutely need to accomplish.

Medium priority: These are things you feel you should do.

They aren't essential but they are important enough that you write them down as a goal.

Lowest priority: These are activities that are nice to do that you can do when you have more time.

Make time for what is important to you and let go of things that aren't that important to your happiness.

7. Write lists.

Make lists for everything. Lists are easy to add to so you have information at your fingertips instead of wasting time trying to remember everything in your head. Keep three main to-do lists: daily, weekly, monthly. Check off each item as completed. Other lists that are useful are:

- groceries
- calls to make
- errands to run (number them in the order of destination and convenience)
- gifts (both those purchased and what to buy including sizes)
- projects
- thoughts
- goals

8. Keep a record.

Keeping track of a task or activity will save time the next time you have to do it. For example:

When planning a party, keep track of who came, the menu served, the decorations, games, etc. After the party, evaluate what worked and what didn't work and write it down.

When you look up a phone number, program it in your phone or enter it in your planner. Odds are you will use the number again.

Create a template for a packing list on the computer. Print it off each time you travel.

Create a grocery shopping template specific to how your grocery store aisles are arranged.

9. Use a timer.

When starting any task you dread, such as doing the dishes, filing papers, or straightening up a room, or any task that you can get carried away with, such as reading e-mails or surfing the internet, set a time limit to complete that task. Set a timer so you know when the time is up and you can focus on the task instead of staring at the clock. You'll work faster when you try to beat the clock. It also gives you permission to stop when it rings so you don't get overwhelmed by a large task. It sets a boundary so you don't spend more time than you can afford, which will cause you to rush later.

10. Schedule projects around your energy level.

Schedule work on physically or mentally demanding projects during the time of day when you feel most energetic. It is much easier to do any task when you have the energy to do it. When you have energy, your mind is clearer, which improves focus and makes you more efficient.

Before you start your work, write down your goals and make a plan to accomplish them. When you feel tired, stop for the day or, at the very least, take a break. Sometimes shifting to another project for a while can renew your energy.

11. Practice saying "no."

Manage your schedule and reduce your stress level by saying "no" without feeling guilty.

- Saying "no" is not selfish. It is a way to devote quality time to current commitments, to yourself, and to your family.
- Saying "no" opens up opportunities for others to serve and learn.
- Saying "no" can help you stay healthy because you won't be as likely to feel exhausted and stressed all the time.

12. Give a thought-out response.

We often feel put on the spot when we are asked to take on a new obligation. Instead of giving an immediate response, set a deadline for when you will accept or decline the offer. Make this your standard policy for all situations.

If you are excited about an opportunity, you can confirm it will fit in your schedule or figure out a way to make it work before you commit.

If you dread the opportunity, you can remove yourself from the situation so you don't feel guilty or pressured into accepting it in the moment. It's often easier to say "no" through an indirect form of communication, such as a phone call or e-mail, than in person.

If you are unsure about the opportunity, you can take time to thoughtfully consider it.

When you have too many obligations, deadlines, and activities, and not enough time, your stress level will build, even if you love everything you are doing.

13. Delegate as often as possible.

Learning to delegate can save you time and help your family members build confidence by learning valuable life skills for the future. When you delegate more things to others, you free up your time so you can do other things you want or need to do.

When teaching children a new task, work along with them until they understand it. Don't just tell how to do it, show them how to do it. They will catch on quicker and you can back away sooner.

Ask them to evaluate their performance of the task and tell them how you think they did. Praise the good; it will improve their skills faster than criticizing.

Follow up with them after they have finished the task. When you and they are confident it is being done correctly you can just do periodic checks. Expect mistakes. Mentor them, don't bury them under feelings of guilt.

14. Give up on being a perfectionist.

Expecting perfection causes a lot of stress, and in reality, it's impossible to achieve.

Perfectionism can cause procrastination. Trying to do things perfectly makes it hard to get started, so things are put off or not finished even though a lot of worry and thought has gone into the task.

Perfectionists often can't delegate or see the big picture. To save time, you need to do both.

Let go of perfectionism by being realistic about your capabilities. Take pride in finishing a project, even if you don't think it is perfect. As the proverb says, "a bird in the hand is worth two in the bush."

15. Let go of fear.

If you put off a task because you're afraid of failure, label your first attempt a trial run. If things go bad, you can try again. If they go well, the task will be complete. Either way, you'll make a start and work past your fear. Remember, worry robs you of time.

16. Make time to rest.

Studies have proven that people think more clearly, have more energy and are more productive when they are rested and getting enough sleep, so be sure to make time in your schedule to sleep. Also be sure to build in some "down" time from work and stress so you can relax.

According to Dr. Herbert Benson, a pioneer in mind/body medicine from Harvard Medical School, "Taking a break causes physiological changes in your body that counteract the harmful effects of stress."

When you rest, don't spend that time thinking of chores or other things you need to do, because that's counterproductive. Remember, in the long run, getting proper rest will make you more productive. You will keep your focus and maintain your health.

17. Take steps to overcome procrastination.

Use these ideas to help you overcome procrastination:

- Start a project when you have the most energy.
- Start with the easiest thing to do. This builds confidence.
- Make a to-do list and follow it. Check each thing off as you accomplish it.
- Set realistic goals about how much you can accomplish within a specific time frame. Estimate more time rather than less time.
- Start tasks when you won't be interrupted.
- Use little pockets of time during the day to get things done. You'd be surprised how much you can advance a project in just fifteen minutes a day.
- Reward yourself after reaching small goals and give yourself a bigger reward when the project is finished.
- Just start! This can be the hardest part. Work in small increments of time to begin with so you don't get overwhelmed.

18. Eat the elephant one bite at a time.

Big projects can seem overwhelming. They're easy to put off when we make a mountain out of a molehill, but feelings of stress and guilt build. Time is wasted worrying about getting large projects done instead of just getting it done.

Big projects are easier to do and less stressful when you work on them a little at a time.

Look at the big picture and break it down into small pieces. Plan a target date to have the entire project finished and figure out how much needs to be done every day to reach your goal.

Start slow—taking tortoise-sized steps. Set a timer for fifteen to twenty minutes and see how much you can get done. Before you know it you will have reached your goal.

19. Be intentional with your time on the phone.

Answer phone calls at your convenience. You don't have to answer your phone just because it's ringing. When you set aside time for a project that needs your full attention, let your voicemail take messages. Schedule a specific time to listen to messages and return calls.

Use your planner to schedule calls that will take longer so you can give them your full attention.

Designate a "phone center" in your home for your cell phone and its charger so you always know where they are. Make it a habit to charge your phone every night. Keep a notepad, pencils, and pens in a basket in this area so you can easily take notes during a call.

20. Take control of your e-mail.

Schedule uninterrupted time to read and organize e-mail.

Start at the top of your inbox and go through each message one at a time.

Create folders by topic, person, project, or other ways that make sense to you, and move messages into them. This will help keep your inbox empty.

Reduce junk mail by using spam and junk filters. When you receive junk mail, mark it as spam.

Flag messages that require action within two to three days for follow up. If you want to move them to a folder to get them out of your inbox, set up an action folder and open it often to ensure you complete tasks.

21. Limit your time on the computer.

Surfing the internet and reading blogs can be a big time eater. Set a timer to limit the time you allow yourself to surf the Internet. When the timer rings, put your computer to sleep and move on to doing something else from your to-do list.

If you have a lot of work to do on the computer, make a list of the things you need to accomplish and stick to it to keep you on task.

22. Consolidate your errands.

There are a few ways to efficiently run errands. Start by identifying the errands you need to accomplish for the week. You can then identify the days you will run each errand, or you can set aside one day as errand day and run them all at once. Choose the option that best fits your schedule.

Always group errands together by geographic location and save even more time by shopping in an area with a number of merchants that meet your needs.

Consolidate trips whenever possible. For example, plan to run errands on your way home from work or before or after you have an appointment that takes you out of the house. This saves time, fuel, and mileage. Frequent short trips can take a toll on your car.

When you need to return an item to a store, place it near the door of your home or put it directly in your car so you don't forget it the next time you are out and about (or the next time you are running errands).

23. Plan ahead to minimize your wait time.

Standing in lines is a waste of valuable time. Avoid them using these tips:

- Don't shop during peak times. Weekday mornings and during the dinner hour is typically the slowest time at stores. Avoid shopping on the weekend whenever possible.
- Purchase tickets online for concerts, movies, plays, and sporting events.
- Schedule the first appointment of the day at doctor's or dentist's offices.

- Make appointments for services such as hair cuts and manicures instead of just walking in.
- Before you take a trip, identify attractions you want to visit that require tickets for admission and purchase tickets ahead of time.

Keep a book or an easily portable project to keep you occupied just in case you do need to wait in a line. This is a good time to multitask.

24. Tailor your chauffeuring services.

Set up carpools with other parents to get your children to school and extracurricular activities.

Try to run a few errands before or after you need to drop your children off at an event to combine trips and save time, fuel, and mileage.

Learn to say "no" without feeling guilty when your children ask you to run them places and it's not convenient for you. Help them think of other ways to get where they want to go. Manage these requests by letting your children know when you are available to take them or pick them up from places.

25. Multitask the smart way.

There are effective ways to multitask. While working on one thing, have something else working for you. For example:
- Run the dishwasher or start a load of laundry while you are doing other things around the house.

- When walking on a treadmill or biking on a stationary bike, read a book or work on a laptop computer.
- Listen to an audio book while jogging or riding in the car.
- Fold laundry or work on a craft while watching television.
- Set the table and clean up prep dishes while dinner is in the oven or slow cooker.

When two *important* tasks are being done at the same time, this is multitasking the smart way.

26. Good mornings begin in the evening.

Avoid hectic mornings by doing as much prep work as possible in the evenings.

- Lay out your clothes for the next day.
- Pack lunches.
- Round up homework and any other paperwork that needs to leave the home. Get backpacks together.
- Take the frozen juice out of the freezer the night before to make it easy to mix in the morning.
- Check your meal plan for the next day. Make a note to defrost meat or pick up ingredients if needed.

27. Use the right tools for the job.

No matter what project you are doing, you save time and effort when you use the right (and best) tools for the job. The workmanship will be better and it will go faster.

It takes more time to try to make do than it does to do it right the first time. Keep time-saving in mind when you purchase equipment or tools and buy the best you can. You may recoup extra cost in time saved.

Also, only have things in your home that work. Toss or recycle anything that is broken and can't be repaired or is difficult to use. By getting rid of the old, you make room for the new. You also spare yourself the frustration of finding something broken when you really need it.

28. Practice preventative maintenance.

Remember the proverb "a stitch in time saves nine." This applies to saving both time and money.

- Take your car for scheduled mileage maintenance to prevent costly and inconvenient repairs.
- Wash your vacuum filters or replace them every three months.
- Change the batteries in your smoke detector twice a year for safety and so you don't have to fumble around in the dark if the low battery indicator starts beeping at 2 A.M.

29. Use labels whenever possible.

Use labels wherever and whenever possible—on bins, drawers, shelves, folders, and more. Though they take a few minutes to create, in the long run, they save you a lot of time. Labels greatly reduce the time it takes you to:

- find an item
- put an item away
- clean up an area
- organize an area

Labels also free up a lot of your mental energy and help other family members remember where things go. Always label plastic storage bins. You think you'll remember what is in them, but chances are you won't.

30. Recognize that clutter costs you time.

You know clutter costs you space and peace of mind, but did you also know it costs you time? When you're surrounded by clutter, you waste time looking for things you need or want. When you can't find things you know you have, you have to take time to purchase the item again. Purchasing a second item adds to the clutter, which then adds to the time you have to spend looking through the clutter. It quickly becomes a cycle.

Cut the clutter by keeping only things you find useful and enjoyable. You'll have less stuff to look through and fewer things to maintain, which saves time spent cleaning and finding places to put them.

31. Handle items only once.

As soon as you finish using an item, put it where it belongs. Dirty dishes belong in the dishwasher. Paperwork belongs in a file or to-be-filed bin. Clothing belongs in your closet or the laundry hamper. Wet towels belong on a hook.

It's so much faster to take care of something in the moment than to put it down and come back to it later. You may think you're saving time by putting something off, but in reality, you usually don't come back to the item quickly and a little clutter attracts a little more clutter until you have a big pile that you need to sort through. Do things only once to save time.

THREE

Entryways & Items That Leave the Home

32. The formal entryway is about presentation.

Your home can be a welcoming place that brings a feeling of peace. These feelings begin in the entryway. This area also creates a visitor's first impression of your home.

If the formal entryway is not your family's primary entrance, keep items in this area to a bare minimum and focus on presentation. A rug for visitors to wipe their feet and a coat rack and umbrella stand will be enough.

33. Make flat surfaces too beautiful for clutter.

Keep flat surfaces in your entryways clutter-free by making them attractive. If the surface looks nice, you won't want to put clutter on it. Place an attractive decoration or flowers on the entryway table and teach your family that nothing else is to be placed there. If this is the best place for keys and cell phones, then contain them in an attractive basket or charging station.

34. Create a home for shoes at the entryway.

Removing shoes when entering the house is a great way to keep floors cleaner. Shoes scattered around the entryway is an eyesore and tripping hazard.

- Corral shoes using an attractive basket or shoe rack. Consider using shoe cabinets with closing bins or benches that provide storage to contain shoes and seating to use while putting on shoes.

- Keep only the most-often used shoes in the entryway. Put the others in a nearby closet or bedroom closets.
- Keep shoes to a minimum at the front entryway. Family members can keep their shoes and boots in the mudroom, or near the back door if you don't have a mudroom.

35. Create a purpose for your coat closet.

Take steps to reclaim your coat closet if it has become a catchall for shoes, books, backpacks, toys, or coats that are just tossed onto the floor.

- Hang only the current season's coats in this closet. Move the others to a different closet and rotate in and out with each season.
- Provide enough hangers for every coat plus a few extra for guest coats.
- Secure hooks to the closet door for children to use for their coats and backpacks.
- Put a basket or shoe rack on the floor for shoes.
- Train your family not to put things in the closet that don't belong there, such as toys and books.

36. Keep cold weather accessories contained.

Keep mittens, scarves, head warmers, and hats in a basket or plastic storage container without a lid. Place this container in the coat closet on either the shelf or the floor. Choose the space your family finds easiest to use.

In the mudroom or at your informal entryway, hang a shoe organizer from a door or inside the closet to hold hats and gloves. Personalize different pockets with family members' names so they know where to return their own items and can find them quickly. Hang hooks on the closet door or wall to hang hats.

37. Keep rain gear convenient.

To avoid mud and water being tracked all over the house, provide a place for rain boots and umbrellas near the front door or family entrance.

- Use a basket or a shoe rack placed on the floor for boots.
- Place large umbrellas in the corner of the coat/hall closet and small umbrellas in a container on the closet shelf.
- If your entryway is large enough and you live where you often use umbrellas, use a decorative umbrella stand.
- Hang umbrellas from hooks in the garage where they are easy to grab and easy to replace after use.
- Keep an umbrella in your car at all times in case you need it when you are already out.

38. Return your keys to their home base.

Keys are important, but they can be so hard to keep track of. To avoid the frustration of hunting for your keys, create a home base for them, a place where they will always live when not in use. Select a location that works for you and stick with it. You could keep your keys:

- in a designated pocket in your purse
- attached to your purse with a keychain carabiner
- hanging from a key organizer in your home
- in a small, tabletop container conveniently located near the door

When you know where your keys belong, you can easily put them away and find them when you need them.

39. Assign a permanent place for your day planner.

When you are home, make it a habit to put your planner in the same place after you use it so you don't waste valuable time hunting for it when you need to use it.

At the end of the day, put your planner back in your purse or briefcase or near your cell phone so you will see it and take it with you when you leave your home. Or get in the habit of checking your purse or briefcase before leaving home to make sure you have it with you.

40. Make it easy to remember your phone.

Designate a charging station for your cell phone and place your phone there every night before going to bed. For a single cell phone use a Socket Pocket available from www.vat19.com. Place your charging station in a convenient location where you will see it to make it easy for you to remember to take your phone with you the next day. If you constantly forget your phone, set a daily alarm on it to ring five minutes before you leave.

41. Set up a mobile device station.

Designate one place in your home as your mobile device management station. These devices include MP3 players, e-readers, or tablets and laptops. A docking station designed for electronics is an ideal place to "store" these items as they will always be charged and ready to go. Keep all cords, chargers, and accessories in this location, and keep your devices here when you aren't using them so they don't become lost or broken.

42. Make a home for backpacks.

Designate a place for children to always hang their backpacks. Label this area so children will remember. If they bring their bags to the table when they work on homework, teach them to hang them up in the proper place when they are done.

Check each child's backpack each evening to ensure it contains everything needed for the next day. At the end of the week, have children empty their backpack of everything and throw away or recycle unwanted papers and trash.

43. Create a communication folder for school papers.

Give each of your children a "communication" folder that always stays in their backpacks. If possible, make this folder a solid, distinctive color so you and your child can immediately identify it.

Label one pocket of the folder "Papers that go to school." Label the other pocket "Papers that go home."

Review the contents of the folder each day when you have at least fifteen minutes to properly process all the papers. Keep your planner and family calendar with you when you review the papers so you can immediately mark down important information and calendar activities.

Put any paperwork that goes back to the school in the "Papers that go to school" pocket. As soon as you are finished reviewing the papers, return the folder to the backpack.

44. Make lunch a snap.

Choose a lunch box that has handles, ample capacity, good insulation, and room for a freezer pack, and that is easy to clean. If you or your children regularly pack a lunch, cut down on morning stress and rush with a bit of savvy organizing:

- Plan lunch menus a week ahead and write them on the family calendar.
- Pack as much as possible the night before.
- Keep a basket of non-perishable lunch supplies together, such as chips, gummy treats, juice boxes, etc. Keep these on a shelf where it is convenient for everyone to see and access.
- In the refrigerator, designate a shelf or container for lunch meats, cheeses, and other perishables.
- Teach children to make their own lunches. When they choose what they want to eat, chances will be greater they will eat it.

45. Create a landing place for work items.

Designate an area in your home for all the items you bring home from work. This could include your briefcase, bag, laptop, and any projects or papers you brought home to work on. If you work on a project at home, put it in your designated spot as soon as you finish for the night so you don't forget it or waste time looking for it the next day. Stay organized by keeping work-related papers and home-related papers separate.

46. Make returns easy to remember.

Designate a "returns" container in your home for the family to put items that need to be sent out of the house. This could include library books, rented movies, borrowed items, or a store return.

Ideal spots for this container are:
- the mudroom
- a shelf in a cupboard close to the exit door
- a container in the garage

When you leave to run errands, put the return items in your car. To help you remember to make the returns, write the places you are returning them to on your list of errands.

If you are returning an item to a store, check to see that you have the receipt before you leave. Keep receipts in a designated place such as:
- a dedicated spot in your purse
- an envelope
- in your planner
- taped to the item

47. Contain pet accessories where you use them.

If you have a dog, the entryway is a logical place to keep its accessories. Use baskets for leashes, potty bags, and treats, and include a towel for muddy paws. If you have a closet in this area, hang a shoe organizer over the door to hold these items.

Contain toys in baskets or bins in the family room or the mudroom, or near the back door. Hang leashes from a hook in the garage or behind your entryway door.

Keep a brush for your pet's coat and a lint brush for you in the same place.

48. Restock your diaper bag after each trip.

When you return home from an outing, immediately restock your diaper bag so you are ready to leave at a moment's notice. You'll know what you used while you were out so you shouldn't need to do a complete inventory. Give yourself time to double-check the bag before heading out the door just to make sure you have the essentials.

Avoid carrying two bags by placing a separate, smaller bag in the diaper bag for your cell phone, lip gloss, tissues, wallet, and keys.

49. Buy the right-sized purse.

If you struggle with carrying too much stuff in your purse, don't buy large handbags. Buy a purse big enough to carry only your essentials. If you don't have room for extra, you can't carry extra.

50. Keep your purse on a diet.

An overstuffed purse is a mental and physical burden. It causes stress when you have to find something in it and you have to carry extra weight! Clean out your purse twice a month to remove any trash or unnecessary items. Less is more when it comes to its contents.

51. Assign homes to items in your purse.

Make everything easy to find in your purse by designating a specific pocket or container for each item you carry. Use a purse organizer if your handbag lacks interior pockets. This type of organizer creates multiple pockets in a purse to help you organize all your daily necessities. It makes it easy to transfer your most frequently used items when you change from one handbag to another.

Keep cell phones and keys in exterior pockets that zip or snap shut for security. Keys can also be attached to the handle using a carabiner or a spiral cord that is attached to the handle of your purse.

Designate a hook or shelf in your home to hold your purse. You will always know where your purse is as long as you put it away in the proper place.

52. Always use a case for your sunglasses.

Protect your sunglasses and make them easy to find by keeping them in an eyeglass case, even if they are a cheap pair. Keep a case in your car and another in your purse or home. Keep the case in the same place so you'll always know where it (and your sunglasses) is.

Keep a spare pair in the glove compartment of your car in case you forget your main pair.

53. Keep things contained in your car.

If you spend a lot of time in your car, you have to be disciplined to keep it organized and clean. Take control by taking everything out of your car. Empty the glove box and all other compartments. Look under seats and take everything out.

Sort the items you remove into two piles: "belongs in the car" and "doesn't belong in the car." Decide on the best places to keep items that belong in the car using the following principles.

Front seat: Contain loose items with a cargo organizer that best suits your needs. These hold frequently used items (change for tolls, tissues, pen and paper, cell phone and hands-free cord). Organizers can be found online at ebags.com, caselogic.com, Amazon.com, and thecontainerstore.com.

Music: Use an over-the-visor organizer to hold CDs.

Glove box: Use a glove box organizer with large mesh pockets or a large plastic resealable bag to organize your registration, insurance information, and other lose papers. Other things to keep in the glove box are a small flashlight, a notepad and pen, lotion, baby wipes, spare change, maps, a small sewing kit, and the car manual. Keep items together in small snack- or regular-sized resealable bags.

Back seat: Use over-the-seat pocket organizers to keep children's books, drinks, and activity books organized. Use an organizer that has a drop-down table for the kids to color and play games on.

Trunk or cargo area: Use a car organizer with large compartments and pockets to hold groceries and sports equipment to keep them from sliding around.

54. What goes in the car must come out.

Make it a habit for everyone, including children, to remove everything they brought with them in the car after each trip. This includes food wrappers, toys, paperwork, and clothing items. The easiest way to keep your car clutter-free is to remove clutter after each trip.

55. Return reusable bags to the car.

Reusable shopping bags are a great way to help the environment, but you can only use them if you have them with you. Always keep these in your car. As soon as you arrive home, take your groceries or other purchases out and put the bags back in your car. Do this before you put the groceries away so you don't forget.

If possible, keep the bags on the front seat of your car so you never forget them when you get to the store. If this is not practical, keep them contained in the trunk using one of the bags to hold the others.

If you have only a few bags, consider using fabric bags that can be rolled and stuffed into their own small holding bag. You can keep these in your purse.

56. Secure sports equipment with a trunk organizer.

Use a trunk organizer to organize and contain sports equipment. Many of these organizers are collapsible when not in use. Select one with either rigid or sturdy wall dividers to keep items neatly contained.

You can use this organizer in your car and in your garage. Always keep your equipment in it and simply move the entire container in and out of the car as needed. Organizing in this type of container means nothing will be left at home that is needed, and equipment won't be rolling around in the trunk or cargo space.

57. Set limits for toys on car trips.

Set parameters for the number of toys your children can take with them in the car during short trips. You'll have less mess in the car and fewer items to return to the house. Let them be responsible for selecting the toys.

FOUR

Collections

58. What is a collection?

When we hear the word "collection" we tend to think of a shelf of figurines, boxes of baseball cards, or a room dedicated to specific memorabilia (be it for a brand or an athletic team).

Maybe you don't have a collection that fits this description. If so, you're probably thinking this chapter doesn't apply to you. The truth is, any group of like things that you actively get more than one of and keep can be described as a collection. Anything can be collected.

Collections can be practical (mugs, books, sheets, china, music), decorative figurines, sentimental (souvenirs, scrapbooks, photos, even papers), or an investment (rare coins, vintage items, art, etc.).

Collections can be great things. They can make a dreary room exciting and inviting. They show off our personality and our interests. They can be rewarding hobbies and give us hours of enjoyment. But to retain their value in our lives, collections need to be actively managed and organized. Collections can easily become clutter and take over a home if they aren't displayed and taken care of (such as dusting) regularly.

59. Identify unintended collections.

Using the definition of a collection from Tip 58, identify each collection in your home. Make this task less overwhelming by evaluating each room one at a time. Make a list.

You already know the things you are intentionally collecting, but what about the things you are unintentionally collecting?

There are probably a lot of practical collections in your house that you don't give second thoughts to—a stack of magazines, hobby-related items, or a décor theme.

Maybe family members started a collection for you by giving you gifts of a similar theme—such as memorabilia for a sports team or a hobby you enjoy.

List all groups of like things that you (or someone else) continues to add to. Write this list down, you'll refer to it later.

60. Ask yourself why you have your collections.

After you identify all of your collections, go through the list item by item and ask yourself why you have these collections. Following are some possible reasons to collect. You may have other reasons. There are no right or wrong answers. The most important thing is to be honest with yourself.

- You enjoy knowing or saying that you have the most or the best of your favorite product.
- It appeals to you visually. You enjoy looking at it and having it on display in your house.
- The collection serves a practical purpose in your home and you use it on a regular basis.
- It's a compulsion. You just can't stop yourself.
- It's a hobby that you find interesting, relaxing, and rewarding.
- It's a habit. It seems like you've always collected the item and now you couldn't stop even if you wanted to because friends and family add to it for you through gifts.

- It was inherited.
- You want to give the items to your children someday.

61. Give yourself permission to stop collecting.

It's time to stop collecting if:
- You no longer love or enjoy the collection.
- You never wanted or enjoyed the collection in the first place.
- The collection causes you anxiety.
- You don't have room for the collection.
- It has become too expensive for you to continue to collect.

62. Make room for new items.

What if you love your collection, but you don't have room for it? You have a few options (pick the one you find easiest to deal with):

1. Close the collection. You are no longer allowed to buy or accept new items for the collection.

2. Purge old items to make room for new ones. If you have a large collection that spans many years, odds are there are a number of pieces that aren't favorites. Sell, donate, or regift ones that no longer light you up. (Even if they were gifts, don't feel guilty. You cherished them for a while and nothing lasts forever.) Bring your collection down to a reasonable number. Then adopt a one-in/one-out policy. Every time you add to the collection, you must also take away from it.

3. Invest in additional shelving. Use this option if it's simply a matter of proper storage or display space—but do this only if you have room in your home.

63. Rotate your display.

Keep your collection from taking over a room or becoming humdrum by rotating the items you keep on display each season. The rest of the collection can be kept in short-term storage. This keeps your display fresh and you may find you enjoy it and look at it more instead of overlooking what is always there.

64. Help loved ones let go of your collection.

If you are a collector, you have a third guarantee in life in addition to death and taxes: you'll receive a new item for your collection at each birthday and holiday. Why? Because they are easy gifts that require little creativity. If we're honest, this is how many collections are started or perpetuated long after the thrill has gone.

If you've decided to close a collection, let all of your loved ones know, and remind them of this before each birthday and holiday. It wouldn't hurt (or be crass) to offer another gift suggestion in its place. Your loved one will likely welcome the suggestion.

If you pair down old collections, offer items to family members first. They may hold value to it that you don't realize, especially if they closely associate the collection with you.

65. Track prices on for-profit collections.

Many people collect certain items thinking they will be valuable in the future. Before starting (or keeping) a collection solely for the purpose of selling it later, research the market for this collectible. How much you can get for your collection will depend on the market value when you decide to sell. Contact a professional appraiser for help in deciding if a collection is valuable. Then stay up-to-date on prices for your collection. If you collect solely for profit, consider selling items within a year of purchasing them unless it's something that is guaranteed to appreciate with age (few things aside from fine art or jewelry have that guarantee).

66. Get professional help when protecting valuables.

If your collections are financial investments, be sure you understand and follow the storage and preservation rules and guidelines for the items. Damage and improper preservation or restoration can completely devalue a piece. Consult professional collectors, preservations and auctioneers to ensure you are properly maintaining your collection.

67. Ask first, pass on second.

Are you collecting things to pass on to your kids? Understand that they will have their own interests and collections as adults. They may not want the things you're so carefully collecting for them.

If you have adult children, ask them their honest opinions on the collection. If they say they aren't interested, don't be offended. Ask if they would want a single piece that they associate with you instead of the entire collection. If you still enjoy the collection, keep the items and designate another way to pass on the collection. You could donate it, leave it to a museum (check with their acquisitions person first), or sell it yourself.

68. Find good homes for inherited collections.

Have you inherited a collection from a friend or loved one, but the collection doesn't fit your taste? Or maybe you just don't have room for all of it. Don't feel guilty. Give yourself permission to let go of the collection.

If this is hard for you, first take a picture of the entire collection, so you can remember it. Select one favorite piece to keep as a memento only if you will cherish the item.

Then, honor the person by giving the collection to people who truly enjoy the collection. Options include:

- giving the entire collection to a family member
- letting each family member select an item or two from the collection
- donating the collection to a group or organization that can truly use it (functionally or to sell as a fundraiser)
- selling the collection

If the collection is valuable or historical, contact your local county or city museum or historical society to see if they would like all or part of the collection. If you keep it for sentimental reasons, display a few pieces and store the rest, but please don't keep the items out of guilt. Your loved one would want the collection to be a joy to you, not a burden.

69. Put a limit on knickknacks.

A knickknack is described as a small, trivial, ornamental object or a bit of bric-a-brac. They're often collected as souvenirs.

Because knickknacks aren't of real financial value, don't feel as if you have to hold onto them forever. If you no longer enjoy a decorative item, donate or sell it. Knickknacks you do keep can be placed on shelves and tables throughout the home. Limit the number of knickknacks on any flat surface to about three to keep spaces from looking cluttered.

70. Protect figurines in curio cabinets.

A figurine is a statuette that represents a human or animal. They're collectable and often valuable—especially porcelain figurine designs by Hummel or Lladró.

Figurines are best kept in a curio cabinet to protect them from dust and breakage. If you run out of space in your display cabinets, do one of the following:

- Purchase another cabinet (only if you have room for it).
- Purge your collection of items you no longer enjoy and adopt a one-in/one-out policy. Any time you add a new item to the collection, you must remove an old item.
- Sell part of your collection.

71. Use custom display cases for small collectibles.

You can often find custom display cases specifically manufactured for commonly collected items. An online search of your collectible plus the words *display case* will likely give a number of options to purchase.

If you can't find something you like, you can always use a general display case or shadow box. These keep your collection organized and are attractive to display. Hang these on a wall or set them on a shelf where they won't get bumped. Use museum wax to keep items secure.

72. Trophies don't have to be lifetime awards.

Trophies can become dust collectors when the recipient no longer cares about the award. Children often outgrow their trophies by the time they reach high school, especially if they were only participation awards.

When someone wins a trophy, take a picture of the winner with it. This will make it easier to dispose of the trophy in the future. You can keep the photo and let go of the award.

Let the person who earned the trophy keep it in his or her room until he or she is tired of it, and then recycle it. A unique way to recycle it is to take off the name plate and make new ones with sticky labels. Give as awards at a family reunion or at a church or scout talent night.

If you find you have a hard time letting go of your children's trophies after they no longer want them, select one to keep with your memorabilia and recycle the rest.

73. Secure china on display with museum wax.

Keep china, crystal, and other fragile glassware in a display cabinet with glass doors. This will protect them from breaking and will keep dust off of them longer. Purchase a cabinet with enough space so the pieces aren't crowded.

Use museum wax (available in craft and hobby stores) to hold in place the china you have on display.

A cabinet with drawers can store fine silverware close to the china. If there are shelves or a cabinet under the display area, use them to store extra serving dishes or pieces you don't want to display.

74. Let go of junk vases.

Many people have an unintended collection of vases. Florists deliver beautiful bouquets and the vases remain long after the flowers have died. When you receive flowers in a vase in the future, recycle or dispose of the vase when you dispose of the flowers if there is nothing special or beautiful about the vase. This will keep your collection from growing.

75. Put your best photos forward.

Digital cameras let us see a photo as soon as it is taken. Immediately delete blurry or unflattering photos you would never waste money on getting printed. If you are on vacation, delete them each evening as you review the photos from the day.

Apply this same standard to your old photos. Go through boxes, envelopes, and albums. Toss photos that are blurry or poorly exposed, and ugly photos you wouldn't want anyone to see. You'll enjoy your photo collection more if it is full of only the photos you love. You'll also have fewer photos to store and organize. Work on this project for thirty minutes to an hour at a time.

76. Categorize the photos you keep.

After you've purged your photos, sort the remaining ones into categories that make sense to you. Categories could be:

- year
- activity (trip, reunion, party, etc.)
- family
- person

77. Preserve your snapshots by scanning them.

Making digital copies of your old snapshots is a great way to protect and preserve them. Work in batches, as you have time, so you don't get burned out. Back up the your scans either online, on a DVD or flash drive, or on an external hard drive. After you have digital copies, you can dispose of any old negatives you have.

78. Organizing ideas for your photos.

After you've sorted the photos you are going to keep, select an organizing method that is easy for you to maintain and lets you easily look at your photos. Here are some options:

- photo boxes (or decorated shoe boxes)
- slip-in albums
- scrapbooks

You can create a separate album or photo box for each category, or keep them all in the same one and separate categories by labels. If you write on the back of the photo, use a pen that is acid-free and memory-safe. These can be purchased at scrapbook or craft stores. Write very small on the back outer edge.

79. Keep your digital photos organized.

Make it easy to find a specific photo on your computer by organizing your digital photos. Select a software to help you. Picasa and iPhoto are two options. Both let you do basic editing and organizing.

Decide how to sort your photos. Options include:

- chronological order (group photos by month)
- by event

Give a descriptive label to each photo folder using the same format each time. Use the date and the name of the person or event.

Delete (yes, I said delete) the practice shots and blurry, poorly lit, repetitive, and disliked photos. Pick your favorites and delete the others. You are creating a collection you will enjoy looking at—maybe as a slideshow on your computer or on a scrolling digital picture frame.

Back up your photos on a backup drive.

80. Regularly update pictures in frames.

Keep the photos in your frames current by updating them frequently. Place the older photos in your designated photo organizing system.

Make the most of vertical space: Brighten your walls and keep flat surfaces clear by hanging picture frames as often as possible. Make a gallery of photos down a hallway.

Keep small, flat surfaces open by placing only a few frames on them.

81. Put old postcards on display.

If you collect cards or postcards from your travels or that friends send you, designate an attractive box to store them in. Store the box on a shelf where you can easily add to it and look through the cards from time to time. Consider framing postcards or displaying them on magnet or photo boards. Switch these out from time to time with other cards to enjoy more of your collection.

82. Keep memorabilia items in a special location.

Almost everyone has a collection of sentimental items. Letters, awards, yearbooks, greeting cards, and other sentimental objects are known as memorabilia.

Any item you keep simply because it makes you feel good or holds a special memory is memorabilia. Keep all "like" memorabilia in a single location that is not on display in your home.

You could use an old trunk, a chest of drawers, or a large basket. Use smaller containers within your larger container to protect delicate items and keep small items together. When you find you are running out of room in your large container, evaluate all of the contents and let go of anything that doesn't light you up.

83. Use archival storage for old papers.

Paper is fragile and can deteriorate over time. To preserve your sentimental cards and letters, keep them in an archive-quality box or album. Archive-quality means the container is free from harmful acids that will eat away at the paper over time. Archival-safe scrapbooks can be purchased where ever scrapbook supplies are sold.

84. Stay current with your magazines.

The easiest way to manage your magazine collection is to read your magazines in a timely manner. If unread back issues pile up, give yourself permission to let them go and enjoy current issues when they arrive.

Gather all of your magazines together and sort them by name. As you do this, decide whether or not you still want to subscribe to the magazine. Decide how many back issues you can realistically keep, and recycle the rest.

Designate a specific container for your magazines and keep them there. When the container is full, it's time to purge back issues.

Contain reference magazines (such as craft or trade journals) in magazine holders and place these on shelves so you can reach them easily when you need them. Clearly label the holder with the year and name of the magazine. Or buy holders that slip into the magazine and place the magazine in a three-ring binder. Find these at office supply stores.

85. Purge your book collection.

Are your bookshelves full of books you hope to read someday, but you never seem to find the time? Instead of looking at your books and feeling guilty you haven't read them, pair down your book collection to a more manageable size.

Collect all of the books in your home and sort them into piles near your bookcases. Piles should include:

- keep
- return (library or borrowed books)
- get rid of (donate or sell)

If you have more books than you have space for, you can let go of some or install shelves or buy another bookcase.

86. Questions to ask about books you keep.

To determine if you want to keep a book, ask yourself:

- Have I read this? If so, did I enjoy it enough to read it again?
- Could I check it out from the library in the future to free up space on my shelves?

- If I haven't read it, will I realistically ever read it? (Tastes and ideas change over time and it's okay to let it go.)
- Was this a gift I didn't want but feel obligated to keep? (You are not obligated to keep it!)
- Am I keeping it because I bought it and therefore feel I must read it?
- Do I have so many other books on my "must read" list that I can let it go?

87. Keep paperback books in photo boxes.

Paperback books can be placed in a photo organizing box to save space and keep the shelf looking nice if the covers are tattered and worn. Label the box and place it on a shelf.

If you have multiple boxes, designate the boxes by category, author, or series.

88. Purge children's books each school year.

At the end of each school year, go through your children's books with your children and remove the ones they've outgrown or are no longer interested in. Donate these books to family members, neighbors, a thrift shop, or a local library.

You may want to keep a few of their very favorites to share with them and their children later on. Remove these sentimental titles from your premium space and store them in a container with other childhood treasures for that child.

89. Keep only the board games you play.

Gather all your board games into on place. Check each one to ensure all pieces are present and the game is in good repair. Purge games that can't be played. Donate games you don't play or don't enjoy.

Designate a closet or a shelf in a closet to store board games. Tape boxes that are falling apart or buy Game Savers boxes. Keep small games, such as dice or decks of cards, in a larger container to make the most of shelf space and keep them from falling off or getting pushed out of sight.

Place children's games on lower shelves that are easily in their reach.

90. Give pens a home in each room.

For most people, pens and pencils are a practical collection that grows out of control. We pick up free pens everywhere and rarely throw out old ones. Place a decorative pencil cup or a small basket to hold pens and pencils in every room. Also keep a small notepad in each holder. You'll always know where to find a pen and paper when you need one.

91. Always label your spare keys.

In your resource drawer (a.k.a. junk drawer), keep a collection of inexpensive key rings that have plastic tags on them. Whenever you acquire a new spare key, place it on one of these key rings and label the plastic tag. Keep all your spare keys in one place so you always know where to find them.

92. Make it easy to shop ahead for gifts.

Buying gifts for others when items are on sale or when you find the perfect thing for someone is a smart thing to do. Keep track of what you've bought so you don't forget or overspend by doing the following:

- Make an alphabetized list in your planner or on your computer.
- Record the delivery date and recipient for each gift on your list.
- Keep all the gifts you've purchased in one area. If you need to keep them a surprise from other family members, use a lidded container that is not see-through. You can keep the container in plain sight in a storage area.

93. Create a gift wrapping station.

Gather all your gift wrapping supplies in one area. Purge damaged items immediately. Take an inventory of what you need based on what you use. If you use only gift bags, then you don't need wrapping paper, but you may need more tissue paper. Purchase tape and scissors to be stored and used exclusively with the gift wrap.

Store all of these supplies together in one area. Two options for storing gift wrap items are:

1. Stand rolls of paper up in a clean plastic trash can that you designate for only wrapping paper. Keep ribbon, tape, and scissors in a box or in a drawer nearby.
2. Buy a portable gift wrap organizer that holds both paper and bows. Many of these organizers include a pocket for scissors, tape, and ribbon.

FIVE

Kitchen & Dining Room

94. Create more cupboard space.

Here are three ways to create more room in your cupboards:

1. Get rid of old items to make room for new. Go through each cupboard one at a time and purge everything you don't use or love. Donate unwanted glassware, mugs, vases, and dishes. Toss expired food and make plans to use up food close to the expiration date.

2. Rearrange items to maximize the space. After you purge, group like items from every cupboard together. Then place these where they fit best and are easiest to access based on frequency of use. Place seasonal and rarely used items in hard-to-reach cupboards. Re-adjust the shelf height as needed.

3. Add more shelves to increase surface space. Removable shelves (available in stainless steel or vinyl-coated metal) help you maximize vertical space. Avoid tall stacks of cans or other short products by using stair-step shelves or removable shelves.

95. Create sensible storage for pots and pans.

Pots and pans are a necessity for any well-stocked kitchen. Here are some storage ideas:

- Nest pans as much as possible. Place a paper plate or coffee filter between pans to avoid scratches.
- Keep lids in a container next to the pans or in a lid rack. If you have room, place the lid upside down on top of the pan and stack the pans on top of each other.
- Avoid deep stacks of pans. It makes it hard to retrieve and return items.

- Move infrequently used pans to the back of the cupboard or to a secondary space in the kitchen.
- Invest in roll-out shelves or deep slide-out drawers in your cupboards to make it more convenient to reach your pans.

96. Designate homes for dishes.

Keep dishes you use most often in easy-to-reach places. Move dishes you don't use daily to a secondary space (higher shelves). Remember to keep like times together—plates, serving bowls, casserole dishes.

Adjust shelf height as needed or add removable shelves to maximize vertical space and keep stacks to a manageable height.

If you have young children, consider putting dishes and glasses on a low, pull-out shelf so they can reach them and help with setting the table and putting away clean dishes.

97. Fewer glasses mean fewer dirty dishes.

Limit the amount of drinking glasses you have. Start by tossing icky plastic ones picked up for free from fast-food restaurants. Evaluate how many you have left and keep a number realistic to your family's needs.

Purchase distinctive reusable water bottles for each member of your family to be reused throughout the day. (If you let them pick bottles they like, they will be more likely to use them.) Use drinking glasses only for beverages other than water, and ask family members to reuse glasses as much as possible every day.

Repeat this process with coffee mugs. If you absolutely can't part with souvenir or promotional mugs, put them on the highest shelf in secondary space.

98. Keep lids and bowls mated.

Gather all your lidded bowls and food containers and the lids in one place. Search high and low to find all of them. Start matching lids to the bowls.

Put orphaned lids or bowls in a plastic bag labeled "orphan bowls/lids." Keep these for two to three weeks in case the mate shows up. If their matches aren't found, recycle the bowls and lids.

Contain the lids you keep in a plastic container placed in a convenient location. If you have nesting bowls, store the lids under them.

99. Zone in on baking supplies.

Designate one shelf or area for your baking staples. Instead of storing them in their original packaging, move them to clearly labeled containers (square containers take up less space). This keeps them fresh and pest-free and reduces the risk of spills and rips.

Use an air-tight container for brown sugar or a specialty stone (available in kitchen stores) that keeps it from hardening.

Separate products that come in large containers into smaller containers for convenience when using them. Store the excess with your bulk items or in your pantry.

Use a turntable to hold baking supplies to conserve space and make things easy to reach.

Store those you use the most in easily accessible areas.

100. Keep things spicy.

There are many ways to organize your spices. Choose the method that works best with both your personality and your kitchen. The quickest way to locate spices, no matter how they are stored, is to alphabetize them. Following are a few specific organizing ideas:

- on a two-tier turntable
- laid flat in a desktop stationery holder that has drawers (about 9" × 12" in size) (Arrange alphabetically and label the drawers. You can keep a drawer for recipes, too.)
- wooden or stainless steel rack that mounts on the wall or a cupboard door
- rotating carousel rack that stands on the counter
- in metal tins that hold to a magnetic strip on the wall
- stair-step shelves

Spices don't actually spoil, but they can lose their strength. Check for freshness by looking and smelling. They should have a nice aroma and vibrant color. Store spices away from heat to lengthen their shelf life.

101. Make hard-to-reach cupboards easy to access.

Make the most of all of your cupboard space by keeping a sturdy step stool nearby so you can access all shelves and cupboards. If you don't have one, invest in one. Use these spaces for things you don't use often, such as seasonal or entertaining items.

For safety, store only lightweight items in high places and don't store treats and items children will want to get into over the stove.

102. Solutions for your lazy Susan cupboard.

Deep corner cupboards are often equipped with lazy Susans to make them more accessible, but heavy items make the device hard to turn, and items can often fall off the wobbly shelves.

To stabilize your lazy Susan, reinforce the center pole with PVC pipe that is split lengthwise and then pushed onto the pole.

To keep items from sliding around or falling off the lazy Susan, place items in small containers that fit the shelves and still allow it to turn easily. Store items that are not used very often on the lower shelf.

103. Be intentional under the sink.

Install an under-the-sink shelf system to add more storage space. Expandable shelves can be adjusted to fit around bulky kitchen pipes. Two-tier, under-the-sink sliding baskets are available.

Make the most of this space by keeping like things together, using containers, and prioritizing space as premium and secondary. Buy multipurpose cleaners whenever possible. You'll save space and money and use up the product faster. Keep cleaners in a plastic caddy so you can carry them from room to room. Install childproofing locks or hooks on the cabinet to keep young children away from toxic materials.

104. Create a useful utensil drawer.

Utensil drawers become cluttered when you try to keep too much in them. If you don't have a utensil holder for your flatware, get one now. It should have designated slots for teaspoons, table-spoons, forks, butter knives, and miscellaneous utensils. Place a mat or adhesive hook-and-loop tape (Velcro) beneath the holder to keep it from sliding around in the drawer.

Use the designated slots in the divider, drawer dividers, or small containers to contain loose items such as vegetable peelers, corkscrews, and corn holders.

Designate a second drawer for large utensils, such as metal spatulas, baking spatulas, a hand grater, and kitchen shears. Pur-chase containers for this drawer or use drawer dividers to keep like items together, and use mats or Velcro to prevent sliding.

If you don't have room for a second utensil drawer, store spatulas, wooden spoons, and other large utensils in an open container, such as a ceramic crock, metal urn, or glass jar, on the countertop or in a cupboard if counter space is limited.

105. Turn the junk drawer into a resource drawer.

Every kitchen needs a drawer to hold miscellaneous but useful items. If you think of this space as a "junk" drawer, you won't be motivated to keep it organized. Change your thinking; you don't keep junk, you only keep useful items and useful items need to be easy to find.

Empty the entire contents of the drawer onto your counter. Sort everything into piles, placing like things together. Throw away everything that is never used.

Don't allow repeats in this drawer. Keep only one of everything (e.g., screwdrivers, scissors, rolls of tape) in this limited space.

Put duplicate items and things that belong in other rooms in your belongs-elsewhere basket (see chapter one).

Measure the height, depth, and width of this drawer and buy appropriate containers. Use an ice cube tray or muffin tins to hold small things such as tacks, screws, twist ties, or rubber bands.

106. Organize your refrigerator by zones.

Store foods in designated zones, keeping like items together. Here are suggestions for each zone:

Door: Condiments on one shelf. Children's snacks and drinks on the others. It will be easier for them to find what they are looking for.

Crisper: Veggies stored here will last longer.

Meat drawer: Cheese, lunch meat and other pre-cooked, processed meat.

Back of middle shelf: Raw meat, seafood, and chicken. This is the coldest part of the fridge and juices won't drip onto other foods.

Front of lowest shelf: Leftovers.

Top shelf: Milk and other large beverage containers.

Middle shelves: Smaller containers. Keep like food types (e.g., yogurt, cottage cheese, and sour cream) together so they are easier to find.

Once a week clean out your refrigerator. Check all containers and toss spoiled or expired foods. Wipe spills as soon as you see them.

107. Properly contain your leftovers.

Always cover food, with a secure lid if possible, or use reusable bowl covers with elastic edges (that look like shower caps). This is less expensive than using foil or plastic wrap. Covering food reduces evaporation, which causes the refrigerator compressor to work harder. It also prevents spills.

Use stackable containers in similar sizes to store leftovers. Consider investing in a nice set with interlocking lids for easy storage in and out of the fridge.

Use clear food containers whenever possible so you can tell at a glance what you're grabbing. Clear containers also remind you of leftovers you may have forgotten.

108. Make a plan to eat your leftovers.

Keep a roll of painter's tape and a permanent marker on top of the refrigerator. Whenever you put leftovers in the fridge, mark a piece of tape with the date and put it on the top or side of the container so you know how long the food has been in the fridge.

Keep a list of leftovers on the refrigerator door. Write down the name of the meal and the date it was prepared. When someone eats the leftovers, they can cross it off the list.

Once a week, have a "leftovers" night. Instead of cooking a fresh meal, clean out all of the leftovers from the fridge and get them eaten.

If you find you are always throwing out leftovers, put them in the freezer or cook smaller meals.

109. Establish a few pantry principles.

Keep your pantry organized by following this checklist:

- Always put like items together.
- Adjust shelf heights and add removable shelves to make the most of your space. Keep like items of different sizes above or below each other. They don't have to be on the same shelf.
- If a food's packaging is too fragile, or too bulky, or doesn't keep food fresh, store the item in clear, plastic food containers.
- Put loose packets in baskets or containers on the shelf.
- Label the shelves to keep everything in their place.
- Rotate the stock, putting newest in the back and oldest in the front.
- Keep a sturdy step stool nearby to reach higher shelves.
- Keep foods you want your children to eat on shelves they can reach. Keep foods you don't want them to access on high shelves out of sight so they aren't tempted to climb.

110. Make a pantry where there is none.

Here are some options for storing your food if your kitchen doesn't have a built-in pantry:

- Designate one (or more) cupboards for food storage.
- Use an armoire or wardrobe in or near your kitchen. Add shelves as needed.
- Use free-standing shelves. Make curtains to cover them if you prefer a cleaner look or need to keep the shelves in another room.

111. Break down your bulk purchases.

Buying in bulk is a great money saver for some people. Make room for your bulk purchases and keep them organized with these tips.

1. Designate a specific area to store your bulk purchases. This could be a cupboard or two, some shelves in the pantry, or a set of shelves in a utility room.

2. Divvy up bulk purchases into single unit sizes (e.g., 16 oz. instead of 54 oz.). Place one unit in your primary food area. Put the remainder in your bulk storage area.

112. Manage your freezer space.

Use containers in your deep freezer to organize bulk purchases of meat and the other foods you keep here. Organize meat by cut or type. Before freezing, separate cuts of meat into smaller serving sizes according to the needs of your family, placing them in plastic bags or other freezer containers. Label the bag or container by type of meat, the number in container, and date.

113. Make a place for paper products.

Store paper products in secondary spaces above the refrigerator, on a higher shelf in the pantry, or in the storage room. Use separate containers with lids for cups, plates, and flatware. Or put each category in its own resealable bag and store everything together in one container. Label the containers they are in and shelves they stay on.

If you regularly pack plastic flatware in lunches, keep it in a tall plastic container near lunch supplies in a cupboard or the pantry. You can easily grab a single piece of flatware without having to remove a lid from the container.

Keep paper napkins used frequently in a napkin holder in premium space. Keep the extra in the pantry or storage room.

114. Meal planning saves time, energy, and money.

Meal planning may seem like an extra chore, but the fifteen minutes you invest every week will save you time, energy, and money at the grocery store and in the kitchen.

Start your planning by noting the food you have on hand. Also check the weekly food specials and coupons in the newspaper or online. Incorporate what you already have with items on special in your meal plan for the week.

Consider how much time you have to prepare meals in the coming week. Plan "quick-fix" meals on days you are the busiest.

If you need inspiration, another way to meal plan is to assign each day of the week a type of food: Monday—pasta; Tuesday—chicken, etc. There are also meal planning sites available on the Internet for a membership fee.

Keep the meal plans on your computer or in a three-ring binder in your kitchen for reference. Reuse the plans with slight modifications to save time in the future.

115. Save time with a master grocery list.

Create a master grocery list template either on paper (make several copies) or on a computer or electronic device. Create separate columns for produce, meat, canned food, seasonings, dairy, bakery, frozen, beverages, pet food, baby food, paper products, toiletries, medicine, and miscellaneous.

Always have a grocery list template either in your planner or on the kitchen bulletin board so the entire family can add items. As you run out of an item or think of something you want, write it in the appropriate column on your list, which you have organized by category.

When you plan your meals for the week, keep your grocery list with you and immediately add any ingredients you need to purchase.

If you have a coupon for an item on your list, mark it with a star or a "C" so you remember to use your coupons at checkout.

Shop with your list in hand and mark off each item as you put it in your basket.

116. Decide how to store your coupons.

Coupons save you money only if you redeem them. Keeping them organized is the first step in having them when you want them. Here are some ways to store your coupons:

- Use a photo album with clear pockets. Slip in one coupon per pocket.
- Use envelopes, labeling each one by category (e.g., cereal, snacks, soaps, paper products). Store them in a shoe box or photo box. Use index dividers that fit in the box to label each category.
- Place coupons in a wallet-sized expanding file. Keep it in your purse or in the glove box of your car so you'll always have it when you are shopping. Label the tabs to separate into categories.
- Use a three-ring binder with plastic sleeves that has nine pockets per page. In the front, put a pouch to hold scissors and a pen or highlighter.

There are several ways to sort your coupons. Chose the method that works best for you:

- by expiration date, keeping those about to expire at the front of your preferred filing system
- by products within each different category
- alphabetically by product name
- aisle by aisle in your favorite store

117. Curtail your cookbook collection.

If you have six recipe books in your home with an average of 500 recipes per book, that equals 3,000 recipes. If you try one new recipe every week it would take you fifty-eight years to prepare them all! Let's get real about how many you need. Give away those you don't use and don't have an emotional attachment to. If you use just a few recipes from a book, copy them, and donate the book. Keep the recipes in a binder or recipe box.

Store the cookbooks you do keep in a closed cupboard or in a bookcase out of the kitchen to protect them from humidity and cooking oils.

If you have a large collection of cookbooks, try putting them in order by category (e.g., Italian, desserts, bread making, healthy cooking). Or put them in order of how often you use them.

Flag frequently used recipes so you can find them quickly.

118. File your loose recipes so you can find them.

Gather all of your loose recipes into one pile. Purge the ones you don't like or can't use. Sort your recipes by category (follow the categories in a cookbook if you need ideas), and no matter how you store them, keep the categories labeled and separated.

If you store recipes in a three-ring binder, use clear insert pages that accommodate index cards (available at an office supply store) and full-size clear plastic page protectors for recipes torn out of magazines or printed from the internet.

If you would rather use a recipe box, transfer all of your loose recipes to cards.

Photocopy handwritten family recipes that may become heirlooms. Use the copy in the kitchen and keep the original with your memorabilia.

Consider creating your own cookbook online with your loose recipes. There are many websites that offer this service.

119. Keep your counters clear.

The purpose of the kitchen counter is for food preparation. To make it a pleasant place to work, it needs to be clutter-free and clean. Follow these guidelines to keep your counters clear:

- Remove everything from your countertops. Identify the items you use several times a week and return only these items to the counter. Find new homes for everything else.
- Declare your counter a paper-free zone. Designate an area for children's paperwork and a landing place for mail someplace other than on the kitchen counter. If you have to keep papers here, use a mail sorter or bin to contain them. No loose papers allowed. They must go in the bin.
- Limit the number of decorative items you place on your counters.

120. Use vertical space to increase counter space.

Make more room on your countertops by mounting items to the wall or hanging them from the bottom of top cupboards. Consider mounting a paper towel holder, electric can opener, microwave, or hooks for mugs, pots, and pans.

121. Don't buy it if you don't need it.

Too much of a good thing is too much. Rule No. 1: If you don't need it or love it, or don't have space, then don't buy it! Go through all of your kitchen gadgets and donate or sell the ones you never use. Keep only the ones you like to use and use regularly enough to justify their space.

122. Keep small appliances out of the way.

Move appliances you use less than once a week to lower cupboards or the pantry. Designate a specific area to keep these together. Install slide-out shelves for ease in retrieving them.

Wind up cords and fasten them with twist ties to keep them controlled. Keep attachments together in a small container. If there isn't room to keep the attachments with the appliance, keep attachments in a drawer.

Arrange appliances to have as many as possible within arm's reach to spend less time preparing meals and cleaning up.

123. Close your kitchen table dumping area.

If your kitchen and dining room tables are dumping grounds for loose items, take control by containing and assigning new homes for these items. Identify the categories of clutter that accumulate on your table and create a specific plan for how you will process each category in the future so it doesn't end up on your table.

SIX

Paperwork & Home Office

124. Camouflage your office in shared areas.

When your home office space shares a room that is used for other purposes, it needs to be compact and tidy. Use an office armoire as a designated workspace so you can hide your computer and the office supplies. Consider using a folding screen to hide office space when using the room for other purposes. Store office supplies on a closet shelf or in a two-drawer filing cabinet that looks like furniture placed next to the desk or armoire.

To save space, use a three-in-one printer, copier, and scanner. On your computer install software that allows you to use it to send and receive faxes.

125. Set up a mail station.

The first step to effectively organizing your mail is to designate a landing place for it. Use a tray or basket to keep everything contained in the landing place. Place mail here until you can take the time to fully address it. This will be your mail station. This area could also include your family calendar, a shredder, a recycling basket, and a slotted container to separate mail for each family member.

126. Establish a system to process your mail.

Wait until you have enough time to fully concentrate on your mail so you only have to deal with it once. As you open each envelope, ask: "What action do I need to take?" You have three possible responses:

1. **Do:** Your response to this mail should take less than two minutes to complete. Do it when you open the envelope. Examples include recycling or shredding junk mail, placing it in the to-file bin, or noting it in your calendar.
2. **Delegate:** Place it in a separate pile for the person whose mail it is.
3. **Delivery:** Mail that needs more attention than you have time for while sorting the mail. Make a note in your planner or on your calendar of the action that needs to be taken. Place it in your action file to be taken care of within a few days.

127. Get your name off of junk mail lists.

Keep paper clutter out of your home by cutting down on the amount of junk mail you receive. Do an internet search using the phrase *opt out of junk mail*. Here are some places to opt out:

- Contact Opt-Out Prescreen www.optoutprescreen.com or at 1-888-567-8688 from your home telephone.
- Remove your name from ADVO Inc. by calling 1-888-241-6760 or completing the form at www.redplum.com/mailing-list.aspx.
- Fill out the form on the Direct Marketing Association's website at www.dmaconsumers.org/cgi/offmailinglist.
- Get off Valpak's list at www.coxtarget.com/mail suppression/s/DisplayMailSuppressionForm.
- Stop catalog deliveries at www.catalogchoice.org.

128. Coordinate your bill due dates.

Whenever possible, work to coordinate your bill due dates so you only need to pay bills twice a month. Try to coordinate these due dates with your pay days. Few due dates means you can pay things all at once, which saves time. If you are comfortable with the idea, set up online bill paying through your financial institution. Go paperless; have bill notification come to your e-mail inbox. Set up an electronic folder for each type of bill you receive. Save any electronic verification of payment in these folders. Or set up one folder for "bills paid."

129. Set up a filing system for bills.

If you still use a paper system for your bills, set up two hanging files—"bills to pay" and "bills paid." As bills arrive place them in "bills to pay" file. After paying, label it *paid* and put in the "bills paid" file.

When you can verify two ways the bill has been paid (with the new bill that comes the next month and your bank statement), the previous one can be tossed or shredded.

Record bills paid in your checkbook ledger—whether paid online or with a check.

130. Go paperless whenever possible.

Going paperless can help you get organized, save money, give you peace of mind, and benefit the environment. Initially it will involve some time and energy, but the long-term results will be worth it. Start your paperless process by creating a secure e-mail account that you check on a daily basis.

Visit the websites for all the companies you receive bills from. Create a customer account on each site so you can pay these bills online. Sign up to receive bills and notifications via e-mail instead of regular mail. Save proof of payment on your computer instead of printing it out.

131. Choose strong passwords.

Going paperless and handing all your finances online is a great way to clear clutter. Every online service requires users to set up an account protected by a password. Create strong passwords for all financial and other documents that need protecting. A strong password is long, has letters, punctuation, symbols, and numbers.

- When possible, use fourteen characters or more.
- The greater the variety of characters the better.
- Use the entire keyboard, not just the letters and characters you use most often.
- Change your password regularly. If you use different passwords for different websites, rotate portions of your passwords every few weeks.

132. Safely store your passwords.

Effective passwords can be very hard to remember, especially if you are regularly changing them. To safely keep track of your passwords, security experts recommend using a password manager software system, such as RoboForm (www.roboform. com). This keeps all of your log-ins in sync. You can access it securely from anywhere.

If you don't want to install this software on your computer, write down your password in a notebook using a coding system you create. A coded system could be to use a replacement word or set of numbers, letters, and characters to represent the word you are using. Keep this notebook on a bookshelf in your office, or in a file folder.

133. Create an electronic file instead of printing.

The next time you think you need to print something you received through e-mail or found while surfing the web, consider creating an electronic copy instead of a paper print out. This will save you money and filing space. Make a folder for each topic you want to refer back to. Copy and paste information into a Word document. Save receipts for online purchases as PDFs and file directly to a specific folder.

134. Find effective ways to share the computer.

When everyone in the home uses the same computer, it is more important than ever to have a system to keep each person's files and information straight and organized. In the main documents directory, create a separate folder for each family member. Also post a calendar near the computer for each family member to schedule computer time to help avoid arguments.

135. Keep your computer files organized.

Most computers come with a few umbrella folders to help you keep track of your different file types—documents, music, movies, pictures, etc. Use these folders as a starting place. Create subfolders for specific projects or activities as needed.

Don't save files loose on your computer desktop. Files on the desktop eat up your RAM and make your computer run slower. Regularly purge and delete old files to make more space on your hard drive.

136. Always have a backup plan.

Don't let a crash or virus devastate your computer. Back up your hard drive at least once a month (schedule this on your calendar) using one of these options:

1. Export data to an external hard drive. It can be a bit of an investment, but if you ever have a crash and need to rely on the external hard drive, it will more than pay for itself.

2. Back up information using an online secure virtual location called "cloud storage." Many of these sites offer a few gigabytes of storage for free and then you pay for additional space.

3. Back up your hard drive on CDs, DVDs, or a flash drive. Keep these in a secure place. You won't be able to backup your entire computer using this method, but it can be a good solution for important projects.

137. Properly dispose of old electronics.

Don't let old computers, cell phones, and printers take up space in your home. If you purchase a new electronic device, ask your sales person how and where you can recycle or dispose of your old device. If they don't know, check with your waste management provider. This type of equipment is harmful in a regular dump.

Keep the boxes in which your electronics came in short-term storage space only until the product's warranty expires. After this date, you can recycle the boxes.

138. Paper piles aren't effective reminders.

Do you have piles and piles of paper you think you need to keep on your desk because you're worried you will forget or lose something if you file it away? The truth is, you're more likely to lose something or forget when things are buried in a heap. Creating a simple system will help you find everything and eliminate paper piles.

139. Create a system for papers that require action.

Instead of creating piles for papers you need to deal with, set up action files in your filing cabinet or in a vertical file system on your desk.

Label four hanging files with these numbers: 1–8, 9–15, 16–23, 24–31. These numbers represent dates. When you get a piece of paper that requires action by a specific date, place it in

the corresponding folder. Address the contents in each folder as
the dates approach.

Papers you can file in these action folders include:

- invitations/activities (mark the event on your calendar
  before you file)
- school events (mark them on your calendar first)
- bills
- anything else that requires a response or action on your
  part

Set up separate folders for offers, coupons, and receipts and
keep them with your action folders.

140. Contain desktop files.

Use a vertical file system on your desk if you must keep some
papers, such as your action file, at your fingertips. Put the papers
in a manila folder and label it. Have no more than five folders in
the holder at any one time.

141. Decisions and actions defeat paper clutter.

To keep paper piles from taking over, you must do two things:

1. Make a decision about what do with each paper you
   receive.
2. Have homes (files) for each piece of paper you keep.

Every time you receive a piece of paper—regardless of what
it is—skim over it and decide what you must do with it. You typically have the following choices:

- Toss or recycle it. This applies to junk mail or information you can access online.
- Transfer the information to your calendar. After you do this, you can toss the paper.
- File it for future reference. Be realistic about how much you actually need to keep and file. Will you really look at this piece of paper again? If you will file the paper, do so immediately, or place it directly in your "to-file" box, so you know where it is.

Make it your goal to touch each piece as little as possible.

142. Make a decision about each piece of paper.

Whenever you touch a piece of paper make a decision right then about what to do with it (recycle, shred, file in an action or long-term file, pass it on to someone else, etc.). Do not make another pile.

143. Establish a plan for tackling your papers.

Dealing with your paper clutter can be overwhelming. Create a plan of attack so you don't take on too much at once and give up. Start with new papers first. This is mail you received this week and any papers from school, work, and organizations you are involved with. No matter how big the old piles are, newer papers take precedence.

After you have handled your current papers, move on to the piles. Sort one pile at a time, going through each pile paper by paper. Tackle the piles at a pace you are comfortable with. Do this an hour at a time or spread it out and work in twenty-minute sessions. Tackle the old files in your filing cabinet last.

144. Get rid of as many papers as possible.

Keep as few papers as you can. Whenever possible, record the relevant information in your calendar and get rid of the paper. If you can access the same information online, get rid of the paper. See Tip 145 for ideas of other papers you can get rid of.

145. You don't have to keep paperwork forever.

Just how long do you need to keep specific financial paperwork? It's a difficult question to answer because we each have our own comfort level when it comes to holding onto things. Always consult with your own qualified tax advisor to make sure you are keeping the right papers for your unique financial situation. Here's a guide to help you decide what you can keep and what you can shred so your files are smaller and more manageable:

Bank Deposit Slips/ATM Receipts: Keep until the deposit is recorded on your statement.

Utilities: Keep one month until you see the credit on your next month's bill, longer if you need to prove residency. If you use them for tax purposes, three to seven years.

Stock and Bond Certificates: Keep the actual certificates permanently and keep related sale paperwork for seven years after sale.

Auto Insurance Policies and Claims: Keep the policy for only the current year. Hold onto paperwork related to claims and accidents for a few years until the incident falls off your driving record or policy (usually three years).

Life Insurance Policies: Keep for three years after termination of policy.

Home Insurance Policy Records: Keep old policies for five years. Maintain an inventory of your home contents and update it annually or after any major purchase. If you deduct a claim on your tax return, keep it with that year's return for three to seven years.

Bank Statements: Keep one year, unless you can get them online, then there is no need to keep the hard copy.

Credit Card Statements: Keep one year, or not at all if you can get them online. If tax-deductible expenses are on them, keep them with that year's tax papers. If they have very valuable purchases on them, keep as long as you own the asset with other paperwork related to the asset.

Tax Returns: Keep seven years. Go to www.irs.gov for complete information.

Vital Records (marriage license, birth certificates, etc.): Keep permanently in a fireproof box. Expired passports can be shredded after they have been renewed.

Medical: Keep records of major illnesses, injuries, surgeries, immunizations, and blood test results, and a record of prescription drugs you have taken permanently. A medical history log, including complete contact information of your personal physicians, could be extremely useful.

146. Create an effective filing system.

Set up an efficient filing system following these steps:

1. Create a specific name for each file. Don't label a file *miscellaneous.* If it's worth filing, it's worth being in a file with a specific label.

2. Clearly label each file and stagger the tabs so they don't hide behind each other. Start on the left side and allow the tabs to move over one slot with each additional file that is added.

3. Don't put manila folders within a hanging folder for sub-categories. Create a separate file instead. Manila folders make it hard to see all the tabs and they add bulk to files.

4. File papers frequently. If you can't, put them in a designated to-file box or basket on your desk so papers are contained and easy to find if you need them before they are filed.

5. Keep your most frequently used files in the top drawer of the filing cabinet. Keep those seldom used in a lower drawer or toward the back. Or keep colors together so you immediately know which section of the drawer to look in for a specific file.

6. To keep files uncluttered, purge them every six months. Also purge old paperwork when you file new paperwork that makes the old obsolete.

147. Select the right filing cabinet for your needs.

If you keep folders of paper, you must have a filing cabinet to contain them. A two-drawer or four-drawer cabinet that is 22" (56cm) or 26" (66cm) deep is typically sufficient for a home office.

If you buy an 18" (46cm) two-drawer file cabinet, check to make sure the drawers pull out all the way. Most don't.

If you currently have a cabinet that holds legal-size folders and you want to change to letter-size folders, purchase metal file folder hangers that are adjustable and slip into the drawers.

If you don't have the room or the need for a cabinet, use a plastic Bankers Box. Use hanging folders instead of manila folders and color-code the files just as you would in a cabinet.

148. Keep a dedicated home improvement binder.

A home improvement binder will help you manage projects in progress and keep good records of repairs and remolding that will be useful if you sell your home. Use a three-ring binder to hold all of these documents. Add dividers labeled according to room or project. File contractor contact information (including license number), estimates, work orders, receipts, changes made to the original agreement, and copies of all permits.

Create a separate tabbed section to record all paint colors used in your home. Keep the sample color cards and record the color name, brand, manufacturer, date painted, and room the color was used in. Also record how much paint it took for that room or area for reference on future projects.

149. Manage your warranties and manuals.

Owners manuals can be bulky. Cut down on their size by tearing or cutting out the foreign language sections of the manual. On the manual, record when and where you bought the item. Staple the sales receipt and warranty to the cover.

Two effective ways to organize warranties and manuals so you can find them when you need them are:

1. Create a manuals notebook using a three-ring binder with alphabetized page dividers. Slip each warranty into a separate plastic page protector. File by type of product (e.g., stove, television, blender, coffee table). Or file by the room it is in.

2. File manuals in hanging folders in your filing cabinet. Create files for categories, such as outdoor equipment, appliances, media, electronic, kitchen, office, and miscellaneous. It's okay to have a miscellaneous manuals file for products that don't fit elsewhere, such as an electric toothbrush, phone, fan, furnace, etc. Make as many files as you need, but less is better as manuals can be combined by type and won't be accessed often.

Keep manuals, warranties, and receipts for as long as you own the product. If you sell your house, give the relevant ones to the new owners.

150. Centralize your correspondence supplies.

E-mail and text messaging have replaced letter writing, but there are still a few occasions when it is necessary (or extra thoughtful) to write a letter or a note. Make it easy on yourself by creating a center where all your writing supplies are at your fingertips.

Gather together all needed supplies—stationery, greeting cards, note cards, postcards, pens, stamps, address labels, and address book. Keep supplies in one container and place them on a

Paperwork & Home Office

shelf, or designate a desk drawer. Use smaller containers, such as decorative boxes, inside the larger container or drawer. Keep only the stationery you like and use. Recycle those you do not use. Keep a supply of greeting and birthday cards on hand so you don't need to scramble for a card at the last minute. You can buy cards in bulk from a mail order catalog such as Current Inc. Update addresses when you receive a notification of a change.

151. Keep your desk clear.

Keep your desk uncluttered by using this checklist:

- Keep only essential items on your desk (computer, phone, in/out box, label maker, a holder with pens and pencils).
- Keep paperwork in files or your in/out box.
- Keep only the supplies you use daily in the drawers (e.g., paper clips, tape, scissors, stapler).
- Limit the number of personal items on your desk (including photos) to three or four.
- Tidy up your desk whenever you are finished using it for the day.

Make working at your desk more enjoyable by investing in a comfortable chair that helps your posture.

152. Add more drawers to your desk.

Need more desk drawers? Slide a file cabinet under the desk or beside it. Or use containers with lids to hold small office supplies, such as a stapler, scissors, and paper clips, on a nearby shelf.

153. Use your planner instead of sticky notes.

Keep your planner on your desk while you're at home. Record phone numbers and to-do lists in it instead of on sticky notes or loose scraps of paper.

154. Untangle those cords.

The jumble of cords and cables behind your desk is unsightly and even potentially dangerous. Eliminate the chaos once and for all by organizing and properly containing those wires.

Power down all electronic devices on your desk. Disconnect all cables and unplug all cords from the surge protector and wall outlet.

Be sure you have an adequate surge protector that can properly protect your electronics from sudden fluctuations in your power supply and don't overload an electrical outlet.

Unwind all cords and cables to their full lengths. Make sure the cords are long enough and not stretched too far. Reattach the cables one at a time. As you reattach a cable, label what it is for (computer, printer, router, etc.) using tape, zip ties with labeling plate, cable organizer ties with color ID labels, or peel-off labels.

Secure extra long cords by looping the excess and tying it with twist ties, hook-and-loop cable straps, zip ties, or electrical tape.

If you have a group of cables moving from the same area to the same power source, tie those cables together every couple of inches.

Cable management trays can be installed underneath the desk or on the wall to keep wires off the floor. Run the wires along the cable management tray and through the hole so they can be plugged into the wall outlet. Or use PVC pipe for a cable holder.

When you are finished securing all the cords, plug the devices back into the power source.

When making future upgrades, consider investing in wireless desktop products.

155. Be energy efficient.

Plug devices you rarely use, such as a printer or fax machine, into a surge protector that allows you to turn off the power so the devices don't drain power while they are not being used.

Don't leave adaptors and chargers plugged into an electrical outlet after you finish charging the device. They continue to draw electricity, even if a device is not attached.

156. Protect your identity.

Identity theft is a devastating crime that can often go undetected for some time. Staying organized may help you protect your identity.

- Shred any documents that contain information that could be used to steal your identity, including your full name, age, birthday, address, Social Security number, account information, and any other personal information.

- Use the same credit card for all online purchases. That way, if there is a problem, you only have to cancel one card and deal with one account.
- Make photocopies of everything in your wallet: credit cards (front and back), insurance cards, IDs. Keep these copies in a fireproof box in your home. Update it regularly. If something is stolen, you'll be able to immediately alert all of the relevant parties in case of potential identify theft.
- Do not carry your Social Security card with you. Keep it in your fireproof box.
- Carefully evaluate your bank statements and credit card statements each month. Immediately report any unauthorized charges.
- Once a year, request a free credit report and check it for unauthorized accounts and other potential problems. The Fair Credit Reporting Act (FCRA) requires each of the nationwide consumer reporting companies—Equifax, Experian, and TransUnion—to provide you with a free copy of your credit report, at your request, once every twelve months. To order, visit www.annualcreditreport. com or call 1-877-322-8228. This is the only website authorized to fill orders for free annual credit reports. Don't be fooled by other sites!

SEVEN

Living Areas

157. Identify the functions of your living area.

Your living area, whether you call it the family room, great room, or living room, is one of the most comfortable and highly used places in the home. You spend a lot of time there, so, naturally, a lot of your stuff ends up there. Make a list all of the activities you do in this room. Do you: watch television, read, nap, eat meals, pay bills, sort mail, work on hobbies or crafts, exercise, or play games? There's no right or wrong answer. Simply identify everything you do in this room. When your list is complete, go through each task and identify all the items you need for it. Then identify how you can best accommodate all of these items. Arrange the room to meet your needs.

158. Arrange furniture around a focal point.

Arranging furniture in your living room can be a challenge, but well worth the effort. Decide on a focal point, such as the entertainment center, a large window, or the fireplace. Arrange the furniture around the focal point. Place the chairs and sofa no more than eight feet apart to make it easy to talk with others.

If possible, place a table by each chair and sofa to hold a lamp, select photos and other decorations. Allow 14"–18" (36–46cm) of legroom between the coffee table and the sofa.

159. Identify your clutter.

Living areas are full of flat surfaces that attract clutter. If you can't seem to keep your coffee table and other flat surfaces clear, take a moment to evaluate the clutter that accumulates there. Identify the items that continually end up on your coffee table. These items end up in your living room because they don't have homes.

If the coffee table is the most logical place for the items, purchase containers to keep them tidy and together. If the items belong elsewhere, establish a permanent home for them and create a new habit of putting them where they belong.

160. Use your surfaces wisely.

End tables and coffee tables can hold a lamp, coasters, books, magazines and a few knickknacks, but we all know clutter quickly accumulates here. If you regularly review mail in your living room, place a basket in the room to contain it. Also keep a trash can nearby so you can immediately toss junk. Use a basket for newspapers, hang hooks in another room for backpacks, put mail in a container in the office or place it in a vertical holder in another room.

161. Make room for seasonal decorations.

When decorating for the holidays, remove as many of your regular, year-round decorations as needed to make room for an attractive seasonal display. You can store your year-round decorations in a separate, labeled box or save even more room by temporarily keeping them in the holiday box. When you put away your seasonal decorations, you can put your year-round decorations back on display.

162. Move things easily between floors.

If you live in a multi-story home, you know that once an item makes its way downstairs, it's nearly impossible for it to make it's way back upstairs and vice versa. Invest in a stair basket designed to sit neatly on your steps. When something needs to go upstairs, put it in the basket. It keeps items contained and is much safer than having random things placed on the stairs. Set a realistic goal for how often you want to empty the basket. Once a day is ideal, but if you find that too rigid, you could empty it only when it gets full.

163. Manage dirty dishes with TV trays.

If you regularly snack or eat meals in your living room, invest in collapsible TV trays. These trays protect your furniture and make it easier for you to eat.

Set a rule that food and dishes can be placed only on TV trays. By the end of the day, all dishes must go to the kitchen and the trays must be collapsed and put away. Anyone who breaks this rule is not permitted to take food out of the kitchen or dining room the next day.

164. Corral blankets and pillows.

Blankets and pillows make a room cozy and comfortable, but if they are left lying around, they make the room look cluttered. To keep blankets and pillows from being left on the floor or all over the couch, place a large basket in the room. Select a basket that doesn't have a lid so it is easy to add and remove items.

165. Be flexible whenever possible.

A little flexibility is key to sticking to any organizing plan. Sure, it's ideal to fold throw blankets before putting them away, but in the end, isn't it better to have them just thrown in the basket instead of wadded up on the couch or floor. Be willing to compromise if it will help your family members straighten up after themselves.

Tell family members you'd be thrilled if they folded blankets before they put them away in a designated basket, but let them know you'll be happy if they simply toss the blankets in the basket.

166. Make a home for remote controls.

All devices seem to have a remote control these days. A universal remote can reduce the amount of controls you need. Use one whenever possible. Label each remote so you can immediately find the one you need.

Make all remotes easy to find by assigning one home for all of them. Use a container that is large enough to hold the ones you use daily. Assign a landing place for the container. It could be a coffee table or end table. Teach your family that the last person to use the remote is to put it back in the container. This is a simple rule that everyone in the family can follow.

Keep controls you don't use often on a designated shelf in the entertainment center.

167. Entertainment centers protect your electronics.

If you are big into electronic entertainment, invest in an entertainment center large enough to house all of your devices. It's worth the money to protect your television, video player, stereo and speakers, and gaming consoles, not to mention your discs.

Dedicate this piece of furniture to electronics only. Keep knickknacks, books and other items elsewhere to make dusting easy. Keep the instruction manuals for your equipment on a bottom shelf towards the back for quick reference when you need it.

168. Make your music collection digital.

If you have an MP3 player, save space by uploading all of your CDs onto your computer. Back up your music collection on an external hard drive and get rid of your discs by trading them or donating them.

169. Storage ideas for CDs.

There are many storage options on the market to hold CDs. Options include:

- cloth or book disc holders in which you slip the album notes into the pocket with the disk and get rid of the hard plastic case

- a CD storage cabinet
- stacked on shelves using bookends to hold them upright

When using book-style cases, label the outside with the type of music such as jazz, rock, or classical.

170. Purge your movie collection.

Before deciding the best ways to store your DVDs and Blu-rays, go through every room in your home and gather all the movies into one location. After you've collected them, open each one to make sure the correct movie is in the corresponding box. Put empty boxes in a separate pile (you may find the disc in another container).

After you check for the disc, examine it to make sure it's not damaged. Discard any that are. Put the DVDs or Blu-rays you don't want in a box or bag labeled for donation.

171. Organizing ideas for movies.

Choose a movie storage system that works for you and your family so you can find the movie you want when you want it and easily put it away when you're finished with it. Here are several different options:

- on shelves in the entertainment center or in a nearby bookcase
- in drawers with the title spine face up for easy reading
- slip the disc into a book or cloth disc holder, which saves a lot of space because you can get rid of the cases

- in a basket or photo box title spine up for easy reading

If you have a large collection, consider separating movie genres. When using a disc holder, assign each genre a different color and place the appropriate color sticker on each case. Use an index card to make a key of what each color represents and tape it to the inside door of the entertainment center or place it in the drawer. Everyone can quickly see where to return the movie after it is viewed.

172. Contain your gaming consoles.

Electronic gaming consoles such as the Wii, Xbox or PlayStation belong on a shelf in the entertainment center. Include a basket or container to hold controls when not in use. If the controls have cords, keep them neat by winding them up and securing with cord holders or with hair bands after use. Designate a shelf or container, such as a photo box to hold games.

173. Organizing ideas for books.

There are many ways to organize books on a shelf. It's important to choose a method you enjoy and can easily follow. Here are some ideas:

- arrange books by category, author, or series
- arrange books alphabetically by title
- stand books upright by height with the tallest books on the left end of the shelf, graduating down in size as they move toward the right

174. Choose a bookcase with adjustable shelves.

Look for bookcases that have adjustable shelves to ensure there will be enough height for any book or container you want to keep on it. If you have only a few oversized books, store them laying in a horizontal stack instead of upright on the shelf. Or keep oversized books on a coffee or end table.

Buy the best bookcase you can afford to hold your favorite books and book collections. If you're on a budget, check out tag or estate sales and thrift stores. You can always paint a bookcase to coordinate with your décor.

175. Give your bookshelves specific functions.

Creating a specific purpose for your bookshelves is the key to keeping them organized. Each shelf could have a separate function and hold different groups of items, or you can devote an entire bookcase to a single category if you have a large collection.

After you determine the shelves' functions, remove everything from them and only return the items related to the function.

Add decorative items to your shelves only if there is space. You could devote one shelf to decorative items, or devote an entire bookcase to them.

176. Brighten up your bookshelves.

If you are more interested in an aesthetic book arrangement than a cataloged book arrangement, try some of these ideas to make your bookshelves visually appealing:

- Arrange books by category, color, height, and type (paperback and hardback).
- Arrange books in groups to break up the monotony of a solid line of books lined up on shelves.
- Instead of placing all of your books vertically, stack some horizontally.
- Intersperse books with photos or meaningful bric-a-brac you cherish.
- Take off book jackets for a cleaner, more sophisticated look.

177. Digitize your sheet music.

Consider backing up your sheet music electronically. When you purchase a new piece of music, use a scanner to copy it to your computer and put the electronic file in a specific folder on your computer.

178. Make entertaining easier.

Entertaining is easier and more fun when you can quickly access the things you need. Keep supplies in a secondary space in your craft area, kitchen, and storage space.

Use trays to make it simple and easy to serve food and drinks. It also makes cleanup easier as it takes fewer trips to the kitchen. If you set up tables, keep them accessible in the storage room or garage, or in a closet.

179. Create a work-in-progress activity center.

Many people work on puzzles or crafts in the living room. Whenever possible, pack up all supplies when finished for the day. If this isn't convenient, designate a card table or TV tray as a work-in-progress center and leave the project on it, but move it to a corner of the room and cover it with a sheet when not in use. Put things in containers as much as possible to keep them from scattering.

If jigsaw puzzles are a passion of yours, consider using a specially designed cloth that allows the puzzle to be rolled up without disturbing the pieces.

Come to an agreement in the family that when a project is finished, all of the supplies are removed from the room and placed back where they belong.

180. Find homes for exercise equipment.

If you exercise in your living area, find convenient yet out-of-the-way places to store your equipment. Portable equipment, such as a yoga mat or free weights, can be kept in a container in some other place, such as the hall closet, where it is convenient to reach during exercise time. Keep exercise DVDs separated from other DVDs by containing them in a basket or a specifically designated place.

EIGHT

Children's Toys & Artwork

181 Designate a play area to hold toys.

182 Round up to pare down.

183 Sort alone to save time.

184 Prioritize repairs on broken toys.

185 Purge old toys to make room for new.

186 Show your children the joy of giving.

187 Set limits with stuffed animals.

188 Organize toys by size.

189 Label all containers for easy cleanup.

190 Be creative when containing small toys.

191 Keep toy containers together.

192 Puzzle pieces sort easier when color-coded.

193 Try alternative ways to store books and movies.

194 Eliminate the toy box.

195 Set a toy limit during play time.

196 Give children clear organizing instructions.

197 Teach your children responsibility.

198 Schedule regular toy maintenance.

199 Create a place to store toys for grandchildren.

200 You can't keep everything they create.

201 Keep photos instead of projects.

202 Keep what is meaningful.

203 Create a file or folder for school projects.

204 Let projects be functional.

205 Rotate your artwork display.

206 Rethink artwork on the refrigerator.

207 Share artwork in creative ways.

208 Create a kid-friendly craft area.

209 Regularly purge your children's craft supplies.

181. Designate a play area to hold toys.

Before you start organizing your children's toys, make sure you have a designated play area with enough space to hold all the toys. If you don't have a spare room that can be used as a separate playroom, designate an area in the family room or in the children's bedrooms for toys. If possible, keep all toys in one area, but if the areas are too small, divide them between the bedroom, the family room, and space in a closet.

182. Round up to pare down.

When you feel like the toys have taken over, it's time to pare down. Have your children help you gather *all* of their toys into their designated play area. Round up every single toy in the house—look under beds, behind and in furniture, in closets, and in your vehicles.

Label four large containers (either bags or boxes) "Donate," "Recycle," "Fix," and "Sell," and set these containers in your toy area.

Sort through all of the toys, and put the ones they no longer play with in the appropriate box. Recycle the broken toys unless they can be fixed.

183. Sort alone to save time.

While it's important to have your children help you round up all their toys, you will likely find it easier to sort the toys by yourself.

You can make decisions much faster alone, and if you sort by committee, you may find your children want to keep everything even though you know they don't play with it.

Put the items you intend to remove from your home in a holding place (out of sight of the children) for two or three weeks. If your child misses a toy and asks for it on a few separate occasions, pull it out of the holding area. It's clearly still a favorite. If the children don't miss or mention the probationary toys after a month, get rid of them.

184. Prioritize repairs on broken toys.

Assign a deadline for repairing toys placed in the "Fix" box. Put this deadline in your planner. If you don't plan it and prioritize it, it won't happen. If the toys aren't fixed by that date, recycle them.

If the repairs aren't satisfactory, or won't hold up during play, immediately recycle the toy. Toys that don't work lose their appeal and will become clutter.

185. Purge old toys to make room for new.

To make room for new toys, let go of old toys. Keep the number of toys your children have to a reasonable limit by purging the toys before Christmas and before their birthdays. As children outgrow toys, give them to a thrift shop or friends who can use them. Put toys you are saving for a younger sibling in labeled containers stored in another area.

186. Show your children the joy of giving.

In your day planner, schedule a time to care for the toys you intend to donate and sell. Plan this time with your children and have them help you clean each toy.

Schedule a time to deliver the toys to a shelter for abused women with children. Bring your children with you when you make the delivery so they can see how their toys will help others. When children see their toys are going to someone who has nothing, it is easier for them to let go of their toys. It's also a great way to teach them service and to remind them to be grateful for all they have because there are people who have far less.

187. Set limits with stuffed animals.

There are many ways to store stuffed animals. A few creative ones include:

- large, lidless bins or a toy box
- a net that hangs in a corner (can also be used for bathtub toys and held in place with suction cups)
- clipped to a plastic chain that hangs from the ceiling (most useful as a display for those stuffed animals they want to keep but don't play with regularly)

Limit the amount of stuffed animals your children have. At holidays and birthdays, tell your family your children have enough stuffed animals and they would prefer a different type of toy or gift. When a new stuffed animal arrives, donate an old one to make room (or donate the new one if the child is not attached to it, but loves the ones they already have).

188. Organize toys by size.

After you've purged all of the toys, sort through your "keepers."
Make three piles:

1. Large toys that can be stored in boxes, bins, and tubs.
2. Small toys that will fit in shoebox–size containers (such as action figures, Barbie dolls, Matchbox cars).
3. Toys with small parts that will need individual containers to keep all the pieces together (puzzles, Legos, Polly Pockets).

This makes it much easier to keep track of toys and minimize misplaced toys and parts.

189. Label all containers for easy cleanup.

Clearly label the top and side of all toy containers. Also label shelves where toys are stored. Use photos if your children can't read or are visual learners. Photos often are easier for children regardless of age or reading ability. It's the easiest way to maintain an organized toy area when multiple people are using it.

190. Be creative when containing small toys.

There are a few ways to store toys with small parts. Select a style that will work for your children and remember to let go of any ideas of perfection. Some possibilities include:

- clear plastic containers
- baskets
- shoeboxes

- pencil boxes
- resealable plastic bags (if this is not a choking hazard)
- clear, vinyl shoe holder hanging over a door or from a rod in the closet (Be sure your child can easily reach each pocket. Keep a sturdy step stool nearby, if needed.)

191. Keep toy containers together.

There are many ways to store smaller containers of toys. A few options are:

- a bookcase
- built-in shelves
- a bin toy organizer system (three angled shelves with open bins that sit on the floor)
- within larger tubs or bins

Keep small children's toys on bottom shelves for easy access.

192. Puzzle pieces sort easier when color-coded.

Follow these steps to keep your children's puzzle pieces from being lost or jumbled.

1. Assemble the puzzle on top of a mat or piece of cardboard.
2. Place another mat or cardboard piece on top of the puzzle and turn it over as a complete unit.
3. Create a unique symbol for the puzzle and mark each piece with the symbol, or X the back of each piece with a distinctive color.

4. Place the puzzle pieces in a small or medium resealable plastic bag—using the size that will best fit the puzzles. Label the bag with the name of the puzzle and put it in the puzzle box. The bag keeps the pieces together even if the box is spilled.
5. Wooden puzzles that don't come in boxes and don't have many pieces can be slipped into gallon sized resealable plastic bags.
6. Teach your family to put all the pieces back into their own bag, zip it closed, and place it back into the storage box. Store the box on a shelf that can be easily reached for those who use them.

193. Try alternative ways to store books and movies.

A creative way to store children's books, CDs, and Blu-rays is in attractive dish drainers or wooden plate racks hanging on the wall at a height your children can reach. This is a great option if you don't have shelves or bookcases. It also frees up shelf space for toy containers.

194. Eliminate the toy box.

Toy boxes can cause more clutter and it can take longer to put toys away after play than using smaller bins where toys can be sorted by the type of toy. Toys can be easily broken when they are quickly thrown in the toy box just to get the toys put away. Using smaller containers also helps eliminate a jumbled mess of toys.

195. Set a toy limit during play time.

Make clean-up easier and cut down on clutter by limiting the amount of toys your children can play with at any one time. Set a rule that they can take out only one or two containers at a time. When they are tired of the toys in those containers, they must put them away before they get out another container of toys.

Or divide all the toys into large, lidded bins labeled with a day of the week. Place these in your out-of-the-way but easily accessible storage area. Bring out one container per day for the children to play with. At the end of the day, all toys are put back in the bin. Each toy will get more play time and children will feel as though they have new toys every day.

196. Give children clear organizing instructions.

If you have young children, you know it's never effective to say "go organize and clean" your room. Children need specific instructions, such as: put your dirty clothes in the hamper, put the books on the book shelf, hang up the clothes on the floor in your closet, and put your toys away.

Children can't remember more than one or two instructions at a time (and many adults can't either). Give the child one task to do at a time and then have them come back to you for another task to do, working up from one task to several tasks until they are old enough to remember several things at once. For older children, have them write it down or have a printed sheet posted on the back of their door and have them check it off as they do each task.

Depending on the maturity of your child, listen to them about what they think an organized room should look like. Come to an understanding of what an organized room looks like. When you need to tell them to clean or organize their room, they will know what it needs to look like when they are done.

197. Teach your children responsibility.

It's never too early to start teaching your children responsibility. Show them how to organize, pick up after themselves, and take care of their belongings when they are young so they know how to do these things as they get older and as adults.

Even toddlers can help put large toys in open bins. Start young so clean-up is a habit they carry with them through childhood, their adolescent years and beyond.

Make them responsible for the things that affect them—their toys, clothes, bedrooms, and play areas. Guide younger children and compromise with older children when needed. Make it a team effort instead of a power struggle. Most of all, give up your expectations of perfection. Let children organize in a way that suits their styles and abilities. Setting impossible standards will make them discouraged and they'll give up. Praise every effort they make!

198. Schedule regular toy maintenance.

Every two or three months, revisit the toy area and assess if the toys are being played with and inspect for broken ones. This is a good time to clean them and spray with an antibacterial spray. Set a reminder in your planner. Make this job easy to remember by tying it to the start of each season.

199. Create a place to store toys for grandchildren.

Grandparents can have unique challenges, including limited space and infrequent visits, when storing grandchildren's toys. Some storage options are:

- under-the-bed storage containers with wheels
- stackable plastic drawers on wheels (stored in a closet between visits)
- a wicker basket with a lid can double as a toy chest and a coffee or end table (also store guest items, such as extra bed linens, if there's room)
- a chest of drawers (or a single drawer) in the guest room

When grandchildren come, you could request the parents to bring the children's favorite toys with them. However, it is fun for children to have different toys at your home than the ones they play with all the time.

When buying toys, consider the space you have to store them in. This can limit the amount and the type of toys you purchase for your grandchildren.

200. You can't keep everything they create.

The first little scribbles your child makes on a piece of paper (or the wall) are so sweet and precious you may think you must keep it forever, but consider this: If you keep only 3 pieces of paper a week multiplied by 4 weeks, that is 12 pieces of paper in a month. Multiply 12 piece of paper by 12 months and that's 144 pieces of paper per year. Multiply that by 8 years of school and you'd have 1,152 pieces of paper per child. This is not counting the extra-large papers they produce with special projects.

You cannot keep all of your children's art/school papers. Don't feel guilty about this fact. Children live in the moment, so they don't always have to keep their creations.

201. Keep photos instead of projects.

If you or your child has a hard time parting with projects and art-work created for school projects (such as science fairs or a history project), take a picture of your child holding the item. Then give yourself and your child permission to get rid of the project. You can keep the memory without the paper.

Put the photo in the child's memory or baby book. The purpose of the artwork was accomplished and there is no need to keep it around creating clutter.

202. Keep what is meaningful.

You know you can't keep everything, so what should you keep? You will know what is most sentimental to you, but here are a few suggestions:

- the child's first try at both printing and cursive writing his name

- programs from school plays or sport activities
- awards and ribbons
- report cards
- school photos
- the first and last math paper of the year
- a special report

Label the papers you keep with the child's name, the date, the grade and the teacher.

For large art posters, take a photo with your child holding it, and after having it displayed in your home for a week or two, recycle the poster.

203. Create a file or folder for school papers.

Children bring home so many graded assignments, it's impossible to keep all of them. Keep assignments that will help them study for future tests in a folder in their homework area. After the unit test is over, have your child purge these papers. If you want to keep school work as mementos from the year, set up a system for storing them. Here are two options:

1. Use a hanging folder in your filing cabinet. Each child will have her own folder labeled with the child's name. When the folder gets too full, purge to make room for more. Don't add a second folder.

2. Use a 12" × 15" (30cm × 38cm) envelope with a clasp; label it with your child's name, grade, teacher's name, and school. On the outside, you could also glue your child's extra school photo. Make it a goal for the school year to save only the amount

of papers that will fit in this envelope. Place each year's envelope in a plastic bin with a lid. Label it with your child's name and place it on their closet shelf.

Either at the end of the school year with the beginning of summer or before school starts in the fall, have the children go through their last year's papers to see if there are ones that can be removed. If you have piles of paper now, sit down with your child and help them sort through the papers to decide what to keep and what to let go of.

204. Let projects be functional.

If you have a hard time parting with clay creations your children make but you don't want to display them, let your children play with them. When the item breaks, which it eventually will, throw it away, guilt-free, knowing the item was enjoyed to it's full extent.

When deciding whether to keep large science projects, ask yourself and your child, "For what purpose was this made?" If it was made to learn or to enter in a science fair, then it doesn't need to be kept when the assignment or contest is over.

205. Rotate your artwork display.

Here are some ways to display your children's artwork:
- Hang strips of felt from a dowel rod and pin art to it.
- Create a mini gallery in a hallway or in their room by stringing a clothes line or ribbon and use small craft clothespins to attach papers to the line.

- Display on a bulletin board or a magnet board in the kitchen or another room of the home.

Rotate the display regularly and let go of pictures after you've taken them off display. Or put them in the child's folder where you are keeping their artwork and other treasures. You won't hurt your child's feelings—they live in the moment and the picture had its moment

206. Rethink artwork on the refrigerator.

Though it's a popular concept, I don't recommend hanging artwork on the refrigerator long-term for two reasons:

1. It makes the room look cluttered.
2. The art gets buried if you put other things on the refrigerator.

Use another area to temporarily display your children's artwork.

207. Share artwork in creative ways.

Don't limit your children's artwork to display only. Get more use out of it by letting it serve other purposes. Possibilities include:

- laminated place mats
- bookmarks (cut to size)
- wrapping paper (store it with the wrapping paper or have your children make fresh creations for just this purpose)
- birthday crowns by using a template for your children to trace and cut

- stationery to send artwork to relatives (When the child is old enough have them write letters on the back of artwork.)

208. Create a kid-friendly craft area.

Designate a craft area for your children and keep all supplies here. Use child-size tables and chairs when possible. It will be more comfortable for them and things will be easier to reach, which means fewer spills and messes. Purchase furniture that is easy to keep clean and to wipe off any spills or crayon marks. This takes the worry out of crafting.

If your children must craft at the kitchen or dining table, cover it with an oilcloth (a vinyl tablecloth backed with cotton) to prevent damage to the table.

209. Regularly purge your children's craft supplies.

Every two to three months (whenever you clean and evaluate your children's toys), evaluate your children's crafting supplies. Throw away dried-out markers, glue, and Play-Doh. Replenish supplies that are running low.

NINE

Bedrooms

210 Identify how you want to use your bedroom.

211 Identify and remove your stressors.

212 Make your bed every morning.

213 Properly put away your clothes.

214 Give yourself multiple lighting options.

215 Limit items kept on nightstands.

216 Keep a bookcase bedside if you love to read.

217 Maximize space with alternate furniture.

218 Contain loose items on flat surfaces.

219 Value your vistas.

220 Declutter the top of your dresser.

221 Decorate your dresser top.

222 Display functional items in a beautiful way.

223 Use an armoire as a dresser alternative.

224 Use benches for additional storage.

225 Create a sitting area.

226 Disguise electronics in the bedroom.

227 Bed risers increase under-bed storage space.

228 Use wheeled containers under the bed.

229 Limit the number of bed sheets you have.

230 Find a convenient place for extra bedding.

231 Make teens responsible for their bedrooms.

232 Agree to disagree.

233 Create a dedicated study area.

234 Set up a system for your teen's desk.

235 Storage for sports equipment in the bedroom.

210. Identify how you want to use your bedroom.

Before you start organizing your bedroom, decide what you want the purpose of this room to be. This room can be your own personal sanctuary from the outside world and a place to relax, bond with your significant other, or just have some alone time. When you know how you want to use the room, you can plan how you need to organize it. Make a list of all the things you need to include in the room for it to function as you want it to.

211. Identify and remove your stressors.

To make your bedroom your personal sanctuary, declare it a stress-free zone. Identify your stressors and remove anything related to these stressors from your room. Things you may want to remove include:

- television and computer
- ironing board and laundry
- paperwork and work-related items
- excess items

In your bedroom, keep only the things that really light you up. Find homes for everything else in other areas of your house.

212. Make your bed every morning.

Make your bed as soon as you get up in the morning. This makes the room look less cluttered and encourages you not to place things on your bed, especially if you love your bedspread. It also gets the decorative pillows and blankets off the floor and onto the bed where they belong. If this is a challenge for you, keep a minimal amount of blankets and pillows on your bed so this job is as fast as possible.

213. Properly put away your clothes.

Make it a habit to put clothes and shoes away where they belong when you take them off rather than scattering them about the room. Putting things where they belong is one of the easiest ways to avoid clutter before it piles up.

214. Give yourself multiple lighting options.

Bedrooms need several sources of light so you can relax in the evening and wake up gradually in the morning. In addition to your overhead light, place two or three lamps in your room so you can control the amount of light you need at any time.

215. Limit items kept on nightstands.

Keep clutter away from your nightstands by limiting what you let "live" there. The purpose of these tables is to hold convenience items you may need while in bed at night. Identify what these items are for you and place only these items on your nightstand surface. Possibilities include:

- a table lamp
- cell phone and holder

- alarm clock/media player
- a photo

216. Keep a bookcase bedside if you love to read.

If you love to read and you have books galore on your nightstand (and on the floor next to your bed), a small bookcase may be a better choice as a nightstand. You can keep traditional nightstand items on the top and contain your books on the shelves. Other items you would traditionally keep in a drawer can be placed in attractive boxes, baskets, or containers that sit on the shelves.

217. Maximize space with alternate furniture.

If space is limited, a short chest of drawers could serve as your nightstand. Keep traditional items on the top and devote one drawer (or part of the drawer) to tissues, a book, hand lotion, and reading glasses. Contain items in a basket to save space for other things you need to store. The other drawers can hold clothing, linens, or blankets.

218. Contain loose items on flat surfaces.

Place a tray or decorative basket on the dresser or nightstand to hold lotions, keys, change, and other items that spill out all over flat surfaces in the bedroom.

219. Value your vistas.

The top of a dresser is a mega clutter magnet because it is a flat surface in a private part of the house. You may justify the mess because nobody sees it, but that's not true. You see it, and it's probably one of the first and last things you see each day. Treat yourself by creating a surface you love to see. You'll feel better about your room and about yourself. You are important! Take the time you need to improve the appearance of your personal spaces.

220. Declutter the top of your dresser.

Evaluate everything you currently have on your dresser by asking these questions:

- Why is this here?
- Where does this belong?

You probably have items here that don't have permanent homes. Find homes for them now in other rooms or by making space in your closet, in your dresser, or in an attractive container that sits on your dresser. Clean laundry belongs inside the dresser. Paperwork belongs on your desk. Broken items belong in a repair area.

221. Decorate your dresser top.

When your dresser top is clear, you can decorate it any way you want. Don't neglect this step. If you love the way the top of your dresser looks, you won't set loose items down on it to clutter it

up. Attractive decorations are the nicest way to keep clutter away.
Ideas include:

- attractively framed photos
- figurines
- mementos
- a jewelry tree that shows off your favorite pieces
- a vase with flowers

If you have a long surface, group items together in clusters.
Be careful not to overload the surface.

222. Display functional items in a beautiful way.

Some perfume and cologne bottles are as beautiful as any figurine. If you have a lovely bottle (or two or three), display them on top of your dresser (or countertop, wherever you use them). Place them on a tray to keep them looking neat and contained. Do the same with your jewelry by using jewelry trees or stands to display pieces while containing them.

223. Use an armoire as a dresser alternative.

If you have limited dresser space, an armoire provides more storage space. They are very versatile and more spacious than many dressers.

Decide what you will put on each shelf (or half a shelf) and label them. Keep like items together so they are easier to find. Contain loose items in boxes or baskets and label the containers as needed.

224. Use benches for additional storage.

Throw pillows, extra blankets, and other extra bedding often end up strewn around the bedroom. This is a problem for three reasons:

1. They can be tripping hazards in the night.
2. The items will get dingy and dirty from being on the floor.
3. The cluttered look takes away from the peace in your room.

Use a storage bench or chest to contain decorative pillows and blankets placed on the bed during the day, but not used for sleeping at night.

The benches can be a good place for premium or secondary storage space, depending on your needs. The items stored in the bottom are in secondary space as these are items you don't use on a daily basis. Books and seasonal clothes could be stored here as short-term storage options. Leave room at the top for throw blankets and decorative pillows that are used daily.

Keep the top of the bench clear and clutter-free so you can use it as additional seating and easily access what's inside.

225. Create a sitting area.

If you have the room, create a sitting area in your bedroom. It can be as basic as a single chair, or you can have multiple chairs or a love seat and a small table. It can be a haven within your haven. This space helps you reserve your bed exclusively for sleep, which can help you fall asleep faster and sleep more peacefully.

226. Disguise electronics in the bedroom.

When space is at a premium and your room has to double as an office, you can still make it a pleasant place to be by the way you arrange your space. Place an attractive screen around the desk in your room so you don't see the computer and aren't tempted to answer just one more e-mail. Or transform an armoire into a self-contained office. When you're not working, the doors can be closed and it is another piece of attractive furniture.

Place the television in an armoire or entertainment center that has doors to hide it when you are not watching it. Store DVDs in an attractive box or basket on the shelves.

227. Bed risers increase under-bed storage space.

If you have limited space in your home for storage, under the bed is a great option. To increase the space available, use bed risers that fit under each leg of the bed. This allows 6"–8" (15cm–20cm) more inches of storage height. They can be purchased at most variety stores for under ten dollars and they make it easy to slide things in and out under the bed.

228. Use wheeled containers under the bed.

If you store items under the bed, always use containers. They keep things dust-free and easy to access. Your best options are lidded, plastic containers that have wheels.

Store items under the bed that you don't have to retrieve very often, such as extra linens, holiday decorations, memorabilia, and extra scrapbook supplies. This space can either be semi-storage space or secondary space if your other storage space is very limited.

229. Limit the number of bed sheets you have.

Be realistic about how many sheets you need. Typically two sets (one on the bed and one back up) are enough. If you must have the latest sheets you find, make it your rule to donate one set of old sheets for every new set you bring into your home.

230. Find a convenient place for extra bedding.

Space-saving options and ideas for storing bedding include:
- on a high or low shelf in the linen closet or storage room with each item stored separately in extra pillowcases to keep them neatly folded, stackable and dust-free
- under beds, using lidded containers that have wheels
- contained on a closet shelf in the bedroom

Vacuum-sealed space-saver bags reduce the size of the bedding so it takes up less storage space. If you have room to store bedding or if you use extra bedding at least once a month, these aren't necessary.

231. Make teens responsible for their bedrooms.

Teenagers need to feel in control of their bedrooms. Letting them make decisions about the room's appearance and making them responsible for its cleanliness and organization teaches them skills they will need when they eventually move into their own home. Explain to them why it is important to you that they keep their room organized. Keep your reasons short and basic:

- A clean room shows you are responsible and that you can be trusted with more privileges.
- Food and dirty dishes attract bugs and even mice.
- Things last longer and are more enjoyable when they are well cared for and regularly cleaned.
- It actually takes less time and energy to put something away correctly than to hunt for it later because you threw it in a random pile.
- You can wear your favorite clothes more often when you keep up with your laundry.

232. Agree to disagree.

For the teen who is absolutely resistant to organize, you may need to agree to disagree and let him hide the mess behind his door as long as food and dirty dishes are properly cared for. You may want them to be tidier and more organized, but if they resist, it is important to be respectful of their space. Even though it is your home, it is their room.

233. Create a dedicated study area.

Teenagers need a place to do their homework. If possible, set up a desk in your teen's bedroom. It can be a traditional desk or something less traditional that fits your budget and needs. Alternatives include:

- a card table
- an armoire
- an old door or piece of wood between two saw horses

Use a filing cabinet or narrow, stackable, plastic drawers if the option you choose doesn't come with built-in drawers.

234. Set up a system for your teen's desk.

Help your teen keep her desk clutter-free by making sure she has enough drawer space. Use dividers or small containers to organize items within the drawers.

Place a container for current school papers on the top of the desk, or put it in one of the drawers. Use a two-tiered container. In one put school work to do, and in the other one put completed assignments. Or, when an assignment is completed, have your teen immediately put it in her backpack.

235. Storage for sports equipment in the bedroom.

If possible, keep sports equipment in your garage or mudroom. If the gear has to be kept in your child's room, buy containers specifically for the equipment. If it's something your child uses at least once a week, contain the equipment in a bag and hang it from a hook on the wall or door. If the equipment isn't used very often, store it in a closet shelf or under the bed.

TEN

Clothing & Accessories

236. Recognize the benefits of an organized closet.

Many people have an out-of-sight, out-of-mind attitude about the closet, but after you see the benefits of having an organized closet, you'll wonder why you didn't do it sooner. Just a few of these benefits include:

- It will be easy to get dressed every morning.
- You can find exactly what you want, when you want it.
- Your clothes will hang nicely and stay wrinkle-free because they won't be crammed or crumpled in place.
- You'll get more wear out of each item because you'll have fewer clothes, shoes, and accessories, and you'll be able to find them.

237. Use hooks to make more room.

Hooks turn the backs of doors into additional premium storage spaces. You can fasten hooks to the door or buy over-the-door models that have six or more hooks on one frame.

238. Spruce up your closet.

As you organize, make improvements to your closet. Upgrade to wooden hangers or slim-line hangers. Get rid of wire hangers because they don't properly support clothes. Return thin metal hangers to your cleaners.

Install a double rod to increase closet space. Use multi-tiered hangers to hang different pieces of clothes on the same hanger such as pants and a matching jacket.

If your closet has poor lighting, consider installing a surface-mounted LED light available at home improvement stores.

239. Create a plan before you begin organizing.

Before you start organizing, decide how much time you can dedicate to the project. If you want to do a complete organization overhaul on your closet, set aside enough time to go over the entire space. This could easily be an all-day project.

If you don't have time to tackle the entire closet at once, set aside twenty minutes at a time and work in one designated place at a time (such as the shelves, the rack, the floor). If you work in sections, work in this order:

1. hanging clothes
2. floor
3. shelves (working from bottom to top if you're organizing one at a time)

240. Get a clear view of your closet space.

The first thing to do when you start organizing your closet is to remove everything from it (or from your designated working area if you're organizing in stages). Removing everything serves two purposes:

1. You will be able to see exactly what kind of space you have to work with.
2. You will be able to see all your clothes and make decisions about them before returning them to the closet.

241. Make a decision about each item in your closet.

After you remove all the clothing from your closet, look at each piece and make a decision about it. Sort the clothes into three different piles (use labeled bins to keep them clearly separated):
1. keep
2. throw away
3. donate

242. Ask questions to decide what to keep.

Try on clothes you haven't worn in a while and look in a full-length mirror. Ask yourself:

- Does it fit?
- Do I like it on me?
- Is it comfortable?
- Do I have any place I can wear it and will I ever wear it?

Don't keep clothes you haven't worn at least twice in the last year, unless it's a special-occasions outfit.

Check clothes for stains or tears and take care of any you find before you put the item back in the closet.

243. Let go of clothes that aren't your size.

It's natural to gain and lose weight over the years. Don't keep smaller-size clothes that you are hoarding as you wait for that weight to come off. Donating these items doesn't mean you are giving up on your weight-loss goal. It simply means you are making more room in your life for present items. When you reach your target size, you can reward yourself by buying new clothes. (You'll have to because you won't have anything that fits!) Keep only clothes one size either way of your current size.

244. Know how often you wear an item.

When you put your clothes back in your closet, hang all of the hangers in the opposite direction of how you normally hang them. After wearing an article of clothing, place it back in the closet with the hanger turned in the "correct" direction. This way you can see what clothes you actually wear. If you don't move a hanger in six months, make plans to wear the piece, or donate it.

245. Give new life to sentimental clothes.

It's a common joke that if you hold onto your clothes long enough they will come back into fashion. Take a look at the clothing you are hanging onto and decide if it is really worth keeping them compared to the space they take up. Donate them to a thrift store. Sell them on eBay. Put them with your costumes and let the kids play with them. Give sentimental items new life. You can use memorable T-shirts in a quilt, tear up old clothes and crochet a rug, make stuffed animals, or use them for rags.

246. Arrange clothes in a style that suits you.

After you finish sorting your clothes, hang the keep pile back on the rod organized in one of three ways:

1. **Category:** Pants, blouses, skirts, sweaters, everyday dresses, and special occasions dresses.
2. **Use:** Work, sports, casual, party, and relax/work around the house.
3. **Outfit:** Hang the pieces of the outfit next to each other on separate hangers or use hangers that have space for both the tops and bottoms.

Choose the organizing style that makes sense to you.

247. Buy less to own less.

Before going shopping for new clothes, take an inventory of what you have and what you need. You'll be less tempted to buy a top if you know you have two more just like it at home. Also consider a one-in/one-out policy. The next time you buy a new clothing item, get rid of a like item already in your closet before you put the new one away. These simple practices will prevent overcrowding in your closet.

We all tend to have our favorite outfits that we re-wear time and again. Stick to the style of clothes you actually wear and don't fill your closet with clothes you will hardly ever wear. Buy pieces that you can mix and match so you can get a wide variety of outfits from fewer pieces.

248. Rotate your clothes each season.

Clothes closets are premium space. They should hold only clothing you wear on a regular basis for the current time of year.

Separate your clothing by season and put the off-season items in another closet. If this isn't an option, put them in a clear plastic container, label it and store it out of the way—in another closet, under the bed, or in a storage room. Before storing clothes for the season, ask yourself if you wore it this season. If you didn't, consider donating it. There's no reason to store clothes you don't wear. Check clothes you are keeping for any stains, missing buttons, or rips. Repair them before putting them back in the closet or storage.

249. Save clothes for younger siblings.

If you plan to pass clothing down from your older children to your younger children, organize them when you swap out clothes for the season. Pull out clothes the older child won't fit into next year and put these in a separate container labeled with the clothing size. Store these in a storage room or under the bed or on the closet shelf of the child who will be inheriting them.

If you don't plan to pass on clothing to younger siblings and you're transitioning from winter to summer, transform any items still in good shape by cutting pants off for shorts and long sleeves off to make short sleeves, or donate them.

250. How to handle hand-me-downs.

"Hand-me-down" clothes can be a blessing or a problem. If you receive castoffs from someone with good intentions but the clothes don't fit you or your style, you're under no obligation to keep them. If they are in good enough condition to give to charity, then by all means donate them.

If you intend to bless someone else with your unwanted clothing, first look over each piece carefully. After checking for size and condition, ask the person you intend to give the clothes to if she likes the items. If she doesn't like them or can't use them, find someone else to give them to or donate the clothes to charity.

The same principles apply to children's clothes that are given to you. If your children don't like them and won't wear them, then either don't accept the clothes or donate them if you're too shy to say "no" when they are given to you.

251. Repair damages when they happen.

Buttons pop off, hems come undone, and tears happen. It is frustrating to plan on wearing an article only to find it needs mending. Often, for the time it takes to find something else to wear, the article could have been mended.

Purchase an assortment of buttons and a sewing kit with needles and an assortment of thread (black, white, red, and cream should be adequate). Include iron-on mending tape to mend rips in pants and shirts. For a quick fix on hems, use iron-on hem tape. All of these supplies are available in fabric stores or craft stores.

Set up a mending station in your laundry area. Place a basket labeled "to mend" in this area and ask family members to put items that need repairs in it.

252. Give clothing back its shape.

Clothing can lose its shape if it's not washed correctly or hung up properly. Try these solutions for rejuvenating the fabric.

If the fabric has stretched out of shape near the shoulder due to incorrect hanging, lay the item flat on an ironing board (or a folded towel placed on a table) and lightly steam the area, holding the iron slightly above the fabric. If your table is wood, make sure you have enough padding on the table so the steam doesn't ruin the finish. Remove the iron and lightly press the misshapen area flat with your fingers.

For a skirt that doesn't hang evenly, pin it at the waistband and at the hem to the carpet and lightly steam it, holding the iron slightly above the hem line. After it is dry, hang it up on a skirt hanger.

There are times when clothing loses its shape because of repeated wear and laundering. In this case, there's nothing to be done to correct it. Donate the item to charity, but only if it's usable to the charity.

253. Make it easy to remove pet hair from clothes.

If you have indoor pets that shed, keep lint rollers in several rooms of the home to roll the hair away when you see it on furniture and curtains. Vacuum regularly to keep the hair down. Cover your furniture with slip covers, blankets, or towels, as they are easier to clean. Train your pet to lie only on the blanket or towel.

Keep lint rollers in your bedroom closet so you can roll your clothes before you get dressed or before you put them in the laundry so the hair doesn't spread in the wash. Keep a lint roller in your entryway so you can remove hair from your clothes before you leave the house. Also keep one in the car to quickly get hair off before going to an appointment.

254. Ask questions about the shoes you keep.

Gather all your shoes (no matter where they currently are) and put them all in one place. Decide what ones to keep by evaluating each pair before putting them back in the closet. Ask yourself:

- Do I like them?
- Do I wear them?
- Are they comfortable?
- Do they go with any of my outfits?
- Am I only keeping them because they were expensive or someone talked me into buying them?
- Do they still look nice and are they in good repair?

Sort your shoes into three piles—keep, donate, throw away.

255. Storage ideas for shoes.

Decide on the best place to keep your shoes. This will probably be your closet. Here are some storage options:

- a short cubby unit on the closet floor in which you place one pair in each cubby hole (or space)

- a two-tiered shoe rack on the closet floor
- an over-the-door shoe rack placed on the back of the closet door, available in canvas or plastic
- a canvas shoe rack that hangs from your closet rod

Exercise and everyday wear shoes can be kept in the hall closet or mudroom.

Keep special-occasion shoes in clear shoeboxes or take a photo of the shoes and tape it to the end of the original box. Stack these in a secondary space, such as an upper shelf in the closet or on the closet floor (in a secondary space that you don't use for anything else).

256. Organize dresser drawers one at a time.

Organize your dresser one drawer at a time. Remove everything from the drawer. Sort the items into different piles on your bed, keeping likes together.

Use drawer dividers or containers if you put a variety of items in a single drawer. These dividers keep each item in its own space and keep the drawers organized.

Use the top drawer of a low dresser as premium space because this is the drawer you will get into daily. A good use for this drawer is to contain underwear, and if there is room, you can also use it for socks.

If your dresser is tall and it is hard for you to see in the top drawer, then the middle or lower drawer would be considered premium space for the items you use on a daily basis.

257. Ways to keep socks with their mates.

To help prevent lost socks, buy socks all in the same color: dressy socks in one color, exercise socks in another color, etc. Wash socks in mesh lingerie bags. Or use Wash Organizer Discs (by SockPro) that you slip the socks through to keep socks paired together when washing them.

258. Ask questions about the accessories you keep.

An accessory is anything you wear to enhance your clothes, such as decorative scarves, belts, hats, gloves, and purses. Gather all your accessories from around the house. Sort them into different categories (bracelets, scarves, purses), keeping like items together. As you sort, evaluate each item. Ask yourself:

- Do I wear this?
- Does it match any of my outfits?
- Does it flatter me and make me feel good?
- Is it in good condition?

Set aside any that don't meet these criteria and donate, sell, or give them away.

259. Storage ideas for purses.

There are many storage options for purses:

- hanging from pegs at different heights on the wall in the closet
- hanging from specialty purse hangers that can be hung on a hook, over the door or on a closet rod

- a large basket on the closet floor or shelf
- cubbies (if your closet has them; stand purses upright next to each other by color)
- clear under-bed storage containers (if you don't change purses often)

If you change purses just once a season (or less), be realistic about how many purses you need or want to keep. Do you reuse purses from previous seasons or do you tend to buy new ones? Sell or donate a purse right away if you know you won't use it again. (It will sell for more money if it's still in style.)

260. Storage ideas for belts.

There are a number of ways to store your belts:
- hanging from a belt hanger on a closet rod
- hanging from hooks in your closet
- placing the buckle over the hook of a hanger
- rolled up and placed in an over-the-door shoe organizer (one per pocket)
- rolled in a dresser drawer using a drawer organizer to store one belt per compartment

261. Storage ideas for scarves.

There are a number of practical ways to store your scarves:
- folded in a drawer (use drawer dividers to keep them neat)
- over a padded pants hanger hanging from your closet rod

- on a scarf hanger with each scarf hanging from its own space

Or you can enjoy the beauty of your scarves by storing them in the open using:

- decorative hooks mounted to your closet or bedroom wall
- a set of over-the-door hooks

262. Know when to retire costume jewelry.

Costume jewelry is any jewelry not made of precious metal or stones. It can dress up or dress down an outfit. Wearing different pieces of jewelry can also make it seem as though you have more outfits than you really have.

An inexpensive piece of costume jewelry is often ready for retirement after one season of good wear. Stop the clutter by evaluating your costume jewelry at the end of each season. Get rid of pieces that:

- have tarnished or discolored because they are cheap metal
- feel flimsy (e.g., overstretched bracelets)
- show wear from lots of use

You can donate, toss, or add these items to your children's dress-up bin.

263. Storage ideas for bracelets.

Here are some ideas for how to store your bracelets:

- Use clear, plastic, bead boxes that have adjustable compartments, available at craft stores.

- Place charm bracelets or chain bracelets alone in the pocket of a jewelry organizer and hang it from a hook or over the door.
- Hang bracelets from tiered jewelry organizers that sit on the dresser. (These are available from container stores.)
- Stack bangle bracelets together in a container in a drawer.
- Hang from a countertop mug holder kept on a dresser.
- Hang them from a wall-mounted mug holder in the closet.
- Hang them from a circle belt hanger on the closet rod or on a hook.
- Hang them on a multi-tiered pants hanger that opens at one end of each bar. Each tier could hold like bracelets.

264. Storage ideas for earrings.

Post earrings can be easy to lose and dangling earrings can get tangled or broken if not stored properly. Plus, it's always frustrating when you can only find one earring and not its mate.

Storage options for earrings include:
- a ceramic trinket box
- a clear bead box (keep one pair per section)
- an earring rack or tree
- in the clear pockets of a jewelry organizer (keep one or two pair per pocket)

Keep earring backs on the earring to prevent lost backs. If you lose a back, you can find replacements in the jewelry-making aisle of a craft store.

265. Storage ideas for necklaces.

Always fasten necklaces before putting them away so pendants don't fall off and chains don't become knotted. Hang necklaces to prevent them from becoming tangled. Here are some options for where to hang them:

- on hooks in a jewelry box
- from hooks on a padded jewelry board that attaches to the wall
- on a necklace tree

You can also store necklaces in a jewelry organizer with clear plastic pockets. Place one necklace per pocket.

266. Storage ideas for rings.

Keep your rings together in the same place so you always know where to find them. Organizing options include:

- a padded jewelry box
- a jewelry organizer with clear plastic pockets
- a trinket box
- a glass ring holder or a ceramic hand

Keep your fine rings separate in padded boxes to prevent scratching.

267. Make a note to get jewelry repaired right away.

When an item breaks, keep it separate from your other jewelry. Put it in a designated place inside a container so it won't get lost.

Immediately make a note on your to-do list in your planner to take the item to a jeweler's for repair the next time you run errands.

Also purchase a polishing cloth for your sterling silver pieces and polish them as needed to keep them looking their best. Keep them in an opaque, plastic resealable bag (available at your jewelers) to help retard tarnish.

ELEVEN

Bathrooms, Linen Closets & Laundry Areas

268. Designate yours, mine, and ours spaces.

When bathrooms are shared by multiple people, create zones for each person by using decorative containers on the vanity and in drawers and cupboards to designate yours, mine, and ours items. Assign each person a different shelf and drawer for his or her personal items.

To reduce clutter, use basic toiletry items everyone can use (body soap, hand soap, shampoo, toothpaste).

Assign each family member a different color or pattern of towel and washcloth so towels can be reused.

269. Make your medicine cabinet more functional.

The medicine cabinet is premium space, so use it to store items you use every day. Group like items together by function, such as oral hygiene, skin care products, and first aid products. If products are all different heights, think vertically when grouping objects. Categories can be kept together by using shelves directly above and below each other.

If you have a double cabinet, organize by "his" and "hers," each using one side for personal items.

270. Safely store your medicine.

Although the cupboard behind the mirror is traditionally called the medicine cabinet, this isn't the best place to store medicines. High humidity and heat causes medication to lose their effectiveness (or potency) before expiration dates.

Store medicine in a cool and dry place away from heat and moisture and always out of the reach of small children. Other options are in containers with lids on a shelf in your bedroom or a linen closet.

271. Give your medications a seasonal checkup.

Each spring and fall organize your supply of over-the-counter medications. Check expiration dates and make a list of any supplies you need to replace or restock. Items to check include antibiotic cream and salve for minor burns, antiseptics such as alcohol and hydrogen peroxide, anesthetic spray for sunburns, over-the-counter pain medications (ibuprofen, aspirin), a cough suppressant and expectorant, sore throat spray, and syrup of ipecac. Make this easy by keeping everything together in one container.

Return medicines that are expired to your pharmacy for safe disposal. Do not toss in the trash or flush down the toilet as they are toxic to the environment.

272. Maintain your first aid kit.

Keep a first aid kit in your home and in each of your vehicles. Choose a sturdy container as your first aid kit and label it well. Designate a specific location in your home for the first aid kit so everyone knows where it is. Keep it in an easy-to-see, easy-to-reach spot.

Evaluate the contents of your first aid kit twice a year to keep it well stocked and to toss expired items.

For a complete list of what to keep in your first aid kit, visit the American Red Cross website (www.redcross.org) and search the words *first aid kit*.

273. Use the vertical space over the toilet.

If you need more storage in your bathroom, install shelves or cupboards over your toilet or purchase freestanding shelves or a cupboard specifically designed to fit above the toilet. They are available in a variety of styles and materials. Some even come with drawers. Using this vertical space doubles storage space in the bathroom. You can store towels, toiletries, grooming tools, and decorative items.

274. Use the space on the back of the door.

When space is at a premium in the bathroom, use the back of the door to double your storage area. Hang an over-the-door canvas shoe organizer with twenty-four pockets on the back of the door. This style of organizer is streamlined so it doesn't interfere with opening the door. The pockets keep everything separated and organized. Store curling irons, blow dryer, hair accessories, hair brushes, personal care items, facial products, cosmetics and other things you use in the bathroom in the pockets. Wash cloths and hand towels can be rolled up and kept here for convenience.

This space can also be used for cleaning products used in the bathroom. Be sure to place toxic items in the higher pockets where children can't reach them.

275. Find storage solutions for your cosmetics.

You can group makeup together by categories, such as all eye makeup, skin (foundation, concealer, powder blush), and lipsticks. Or group together by usage, such as day, office, evening, and special occasion. Use what works for you. Following are specific storage solutions for cosmetics:

Drawers: Use clear plastic organizers with dividers to separate and organize. In deep drawers, use organizers that can be stacked. Or use several small, plastic baskets that fit in your drawer.

Countertop: Use decorative baskets, placing in them smaller containers, such as mugs or glasses, to organize brushes, pencils, and mascaras. Use shallow cups and small baskets for eye shadows, lipsticks, and other small items. Or purchase a cosmetic carousel that keeps everything at your fingertips and everything can be seen.

On the go: Makeup bags are perfect for holding cosmetics in your purse. If you use the same items every day, keep duplicates in your bag and at home so you don't have to transfer them.

276. Keep only the cosmetics you use.

Many women have a collection of cosmetics they rarely use. Give yourself permission to get rid of colors and products that didn't work for your or that you grew tired of.

Although there are no official "use by" guidelines in the United States, cosmetics can expire and go bad. Bacteria can grow in them. Here are some basic shelf-life guidelines for safely using cosmetics:

Mascara: three to six months
Eye and lip pencils: three to five years
Oil-free foundation (cream): one year
Compact foundation: eighteen months
Concealer: twelve to eighteen months
Powder: two years
Lipstick and lip liner: two years
Lip gloss: eighteen to twenty-four months
Nail color: one year

277. Keep rarely used items separate.

If you have a collection of "evening only" cosmetics you rarely use, keep it in a separate cosmetic bag in your secondary space, such as the back of the drawer or in the organizer on the back of the bathroom door. Do the same with products you only use when you travel.

278. Structure your under-the-sink area.

Keep the cupboard under your sink organized and maximize the space by installing slide-out shelves or stacking bins. Use containers for smaller items placed on the shelves or in the bins. Removable shelves can also be placed in the cupboard to create more space.

Install hooks to hang blow dryers and curling/flat irons. Tame the cords with hair ties (which are stronger and last longer than elastic bands).

Keep all cleaning products together in one tote. Be sure the cupboard is secure if young children are in the home. Revisit this cupboard about every three months to keep it clutter-free.

279. Curtain off exposed pipes.

If your sink isn't set in a vanity, you can still take advantage of the storage space under it. Attach a curtain around the sink to close the area off and then organize the space as you would a cupboard.

280. Have a plan for sample-sized products.

Before you take home travel-sized toiletries from a hotel, have a plan for how you will use them. When you have a plan in place, be realistic about how much you need for this plan. You don't have to take something just because it's "free." Two possible uses are for:

1. overnight guests (store in the guest bedroom or guest bathroom, if possible)

2. travel (store in quart-sized resealable plastic bags with your luggage)

281. Keep extra toilet paper accessible.

Organizing toilet tissue might not seem like a big deal, but if you or a guest runs out, you'll suddenly realize how important it is. Store the bulk of your toilet paper in a linen closet or with your other bulk items. Keep three or four extra rolls in the bathroom using one of these options:

- under the sink
- in an open basket near the toilet
- in a free-standing tower specifically made to hold toilet paper

Buy tissue that fits into any holder you chose to use. Double rolls or extra large rolls may be too wide to fit certain holders.

282. Make a place for products in the bathtub.

To keep products from taking over the shower area, install a caddy that hangs from the shower head, or over the shower door. Set a limit that the only products allowed in the tub are those that are kept in the caddy.

If you have a tub only, install a tension pole bath caddy in the corner or install a corner shelf caddy.

283. Stop product buildup.

Half-used shampoos, conditioners, cosmetics, soaps, and other products can take over a bathroom. Get rid of the excess products and keep the problem from returning by following these guidelines:

- If you try a new product and don't like it, get rid of it immediately. Either return it, give it away, or throw it away.
- Buy smaller-sized shampoo, conditioner, and body wash if you like to change products often.

- Stop saving half-used products. Use them up or get rid of them before you open a new bottle.
- Instead of keeping super-sized bottles in the tub/shower, pour some of the contents into a smaller bottle for daily use and store the rest under the vanity. Refill as needed.

284. Protect your bath products.

Bath salts and scrubs that aren't used weekly are two products that shouldn't be kept in the bathtub, or even in the bathroom. The humidity will quickly ruin them. Store these soaks in the linen closet and get them out only when needed.

285. Make the bathroom child friendly.

Keep your young children safe in the bathroom and make it easy for them to reach things by following this guidelines:

- Place a bumper (protector) over the bathtub spout and faucets to protect against bumps.
- Use woven or rubber bath mats near the tub and sink to prevent slips on wet floors.
- Keep a child-size stepstool so children can reach the sink.
- Install repositioning hooks (attached with suction cups) at children's height for towels.
- Keep shampoo and conditioner where children can't easily reach them in the tub or shower.
- Install childproof locks on the doors to keep them out of cleaning supplies and medicines.

286. Keep tub toys together and dry.

Toys are a necessity for children's bath time. Here are some ideas for how to keep them clean and organized:

- Limit the number of toys allowed.
- Select waterproof toys that will dry quickly.
- Drain all water from squirt toys after each bath to keep mold from growing inside of them.
- Teach your children to rinse, dry and put away toys at the end of a bath.
- Store toys in a container under the sink or in a mesh bag hanging from suction cups on the wall over the tub.

287. Keep your countertops clear.

When possible, store the majority of your items out of sight in drawers or cupboards. Place items you must keep on the counter in attractive containers. You can see what you have and it keeps everything organized. Keep like items together in the different baskets.

Place toothbrushes in holders (use the open style to prevent mold and bacteria). Use a soap dish to keep the counter clean, or switch to liquid soap in a pump bottle.

288. Contain the clutter between cleanings.

The morning rush and bedtime fatigue can make it hard to keep the bathroom counters tidy. Use baskets on the countertop as catch-alls for things you don't have time to properly put away.

Then put everything away once a week when you clean the room. Place baskets on the counter for miscellaneous items that are used most often but don't always fit in drawers.

289. Do a quick clean after each use.

A few standing rules will keep your bathroom tidy between weekly cleanings. Keep disposable wipes convenient in the bathroom so each person can wipe up small messes right away. After each use:

- hang up towels
- put items away
- rinse out the sink to remove globs of toothpaste and soap scum
- use a squeegee or a cloth to wipe shower walls (reduces risk of mildew and scaling on glass doors)

290. Soak showerheads in vinegar.

If you notice a decrease in water pressure, remove the showerhead and check it for hard water buildup. Do the same for the faucets in the sink. Soak in vinegar to remove buildup.

291. Control moisture to keep mildew away.

To prevent mildew and mold, use the ceiling fan or crack a window when taking a bath or a shower (this also helps control moisture). Leave the fan on or the window open for fifteen minutes after you finish bathing. Spread shower curtains open so they can dry completely.

292. Keep like items together in the linen closet.

The easiest way to keep your linen closet organized is to keep like items together. Use containers, such as baskets, for the categories. Assign each category to a specific shelf and label the shelves.

Keep premium and secondary space in mind. Put items you use frequently on premium, easy-to-reach shelves. High and low shelves are secondary spaces perfect for items you don't use as often. Keep the items you use on a weekly basis in the most accessible areas (premium space).

293. Keep towels where you use them.

Instead of storing all your towels in the linen closet, you may find it more convenient to keep them where you use them.

Roll up hand towels and wash cloths and place them in an attractive basket on the vanity or on shelves in the bathroom, and store bath towels in a bathroom cupboard.

Place towels reserved for guests with the guest sheets. Either put these in a covered container under the guest bed or on a low shelf in the linen closet.

Keep beach towels behind the bath towels or on a higher shelf with other seasonal items.

294. Spruce up your laundry area.

Laundry rooms are often catchall rooms for clutter because guests never see them and no one spends extra time in them. Paint the walls a color you love. Hang a picture on the wall and put a nice nonslip rug on the floor. If you find the room attractive, you'll be more motivated to keep it organized and looking neat.

295. Contain your laundry supplies.

Keep your laundry room attractive and functional. Use plastic baskets or stainless steel wire baskets to keep things organized.

Place small items (e.g., stain stick, stain spray, scrub brush, dryer sheets, measuring cups) in baskets inside the cupboards over the washer and dryer along with the bleach, fabric softener, and laundry soap over the washer in the cabinet.

If you have no cupboards, place the containers on top of the counter or on shelves attached to the wall above the washer and dryer. Or attach a three-tier hanging metal basket from the ceiling to hold laundry supplies.

If you have a laundry nook, use bifold cabinet doors to keep the washer and dryer hidden. Put laundry cleaning supplies on shelves or in cabinets above the washer and dryer.

296. Premeasure supplies for the Laundromat.

If you use a Laundromat, make up single-use packets of soap in plastic bags. Put bleach in a smaller container, enough for that day's laundry. You'll have less to lug around.

297. Shrink your laundry piles.

Here are some ways to reduce the amount of laundry your family creates each week:

1. Ask children (and adults) to re-wear clothing that isn't soiled, sweaty, or smelly. Teach them to put away clothes that aren't dirty instead of throwing them on the floor or in the hamper to be washed every time they are worn.

2. Put a bib or child-size apron on young children when they eat so they don't have to change clothes after eating.

4. Encourage children to eat only at the table to reduce dropped food and spills on clothes.

5. A tiny spot on clothing can be spot cleaned with water, a little soap, and a cloth instead of tossing the garment in the hamper.

6. Assign family members to wash their own clothes. Once they realize how often they'll need to do laundry, they will cut back on changing their clothing during the day—or will re-wear clothing more often.

7. Depending on your lifestyle, wash your sheets on the average of once a week. If you shower at night—every two weeks should be sufficient.

8. Reuse bath towels as much as possible.

298. Make it easy to corral dirty laundry.

Dirty clothes thrown on the floor is not an alternative form of carpet. The traditional laundry hamper is one way to corral dirty laundry until washing day. Place laundry hampers (or space-saving alternatives, such as mesh laundry bags) in every room where people undress, to make it easy for everyone to properly manage dirty laundry. Keep lids off hampers to make it easy to put dirty clothes in them.

Never put wet clothing, towels, or washcloths in a hamper. They can mildew.

299. Set a laundry schedule.

Plan laundry time into your schedule. Wash clothes when the timing is right for you during the day. There's no right or wrong schedule. You could:

- do all your laundry on one day
- wash one load each day if your household has a high volume of laundry
- wash two to three loads in the morning or at night if this works best for you

Let your family know the laundry schedule by marking it on the family calendar. Teach them to be responsible to take their clothes to the laundry room. If they don't, they won't have clean clothes unless they wash them themselves.

300. Start a laundry lost-and-found.

Put a container labeled "lost-and-found" near the washer and dryer. Turn pockets out before washing and place the found contents in this container. Have another container for odd socks.

If the odd sock isn't found in a month, throw it away. (Or make sock puppets.)

301. Make room for line-drying.

Install a hanging rod above the washer and dryer or use a free-standing rack to hang clothes that need to air-dry. You could also install a clothesline that runs across the room.

Do not keep clean clothes in the laundry room. Use separate laundry baskets for each family member and have each person responsible for putting away his clothes. As soon as air-dried clothes are dry, they need to be put away.

302. Make ironing as easy as possible.

Today, many fabrics and garments are "wrinkle free," so your pile of ironing probably isn't too big. Keep your ironing supplies in the laundry room if possible. If there's no room for the ironing board in the laundry area, keep the board in a closet in or near the room where you iron. Or use a smaller ironing board designed to sit on top of a table.

Here are some ideas on to make ironing as easy as possible:

- Remove clothes from the dryer as soon as they are dry and immediately hang them up or fold them to avoid unnecessary wrinkles.
- Do your ironing in batches.
- Check each garment's tag for care instructions and put them in order from lowest heat setting to highest. Turn

on the iron to the proper temperature for the lowest-setting garment and work your way through the pile, turning the heat up as needed as you work through your pile.

- Hang or fold garments immediately after ironing.
- Consider using a garment steamer to remove wrinkles from fabrics too delicate to iron.

TWELVE

Crafts & Hobbies

303. Rethink your craft-supply shelves.

When reorganizing shelves, start by clearing everything off of them. Sort the contents of the shelves into groups of like items. Then go through each group and get rid of stuff you don't want or need. Find appropriate containers for each group, and label the containers. Finally, put the containers back on the shelves and label each shelf. Avoid storing loose items on shelves whenever possible. Containers maximize space and keep things together, making them easier to find.

If you need additional shelves, consider using a bookcase or having shelves built in your room or purchase portable shelving. Use an old dresser or armoire to give you more storage space.

304. Put back what you take out.

When you are finished crafting for the day, take five to ten minutes to put everything back where it belongs. It's the easiest way to keep track of your supplies. You'll gain this time back the next time you work on your craft because you can jump right into your project without hunting for supplies. If you plan on coming back to the same project the next day, tidy up your supplies on your table to make it easy and to save time the next day.

305. Keep project materials together.

When working on a project that you move from place to place, keep all supplies used for that project together in a shallow basket. Your project can then be easily transported from place to place and nothing will be misplaced. When finished, be sure to return tools and leftover material to their permanent homes.

306. Make your supplies mobile.

For easy setup and cleanup, keep your supplies in a set of drawers that has wheels. This is ideal as it can be moved anywhere, so you have everything where you want it, when you want it, but can easily move it out of the way when you need to.

307. Brighten up your space.

Good lighting is important when crafting. A lamp that clamps on each side of your table will give you good light. Some halogen lamps include a magnifier, a handy two-in-one that will save space and spare eye strain. Consider installing track lighting or use a table top OttLite or an OttLite floor lamp to improve lighting. Use daylight or spectrum bulbs so you can see the colors as true as possible.

308. Organize new supplies immediately.

When you buy new craft supplies, put them in the appropriate storage container as soon as you get them home. If you leave them in the store bag, you'll forget what's in the bag and end up opening it countless times to see what is there. (We all forget what is in closed bags.) The bag can also get misplaced and you'll waste time looking for it or forget you have it and make a duplicate purchase.

309. Know when enough is enough.

Buy what you need and use what you buy. Shopping sales is a great way to save money, but buying more than you will use leads to clutter. It is a good thing to have a stash of crafting supplies, but be realistic on just how large of a stash you truly need.

310. Contain your resource magazines.

Keep craft magazines you reference for crafting in magazine holders and store these in your crafting area. Label the magazine holder with the magazine's name and the year.

Start a file for articles you want to reference for specific projects. In a computer file or on a 3" × 5" (8cm × 13cm) card, write the magazine name, year, month, and page number. If you use the card system, keep a file box next to your magazines for the cards.

311. Don't let duplicates steal your space.

As you evaluate all of your craft supplies, identify duplicate items. Do you really need two of the same item? If you don't, donate the duplicates to someone who can use them. Get rid of things you don't like, use, or want. This will free up space for the things you like and use regularly.

312. Swap for new supplies.

If you have unwanted or duplicate supplies, host a swap with friends and family who enjoy the same hobby. Serve refreshments and have a fun afternoon swapping supplies and sharing ideas. If there are any supplies left over at the end, donate them to organizations that can use them.

313. Purge your supplies once a year.

If you don't craft on a regular basis, schedule one day a year to purge your supplies. Toss out past-their-prime materials, such as dried glues and markers or separated paints. If you need more supplies, write it on a to-do list so you'll remember to pick up more when running errands. Keep up with your supplies to ensure everything is usable and enjoyable when you are ready to be creative.

314. Let go of lingering projects.

Every six months, evaluate projects in progress and set deadlines for completion, or give them up if you've lost interest.

Let go of projects you started and have never finished or those you bought the supplies for and no longer want to make. Donate these supplies to friends or organizations who can use them.

If you have a hard time letting go of a big project yet you don't want to make it, compromise by making a smaller version, such as a table topper instead of a full quilt. Then donate the leftover supplies.

Let go of the guilt; you will feel better and this will free up space for things you do like and want to make.

315. Protect your work surface when beading.

To prevent beads and stones from bouncing around and wires from flying to the floor, use a protective mat on your work surface. Some mat options include:

- a folded hand towel
- a "beader's mat"
- a cushion-style mouse pad
- a woven, rubber shelf liner cut to the size of your working area

316. Cover the carpet for easy cleanup.

If your creative space is carpeted, place a rubber mat under your work area. You can quickly pick up small stones and loose pieces of wire before they become hidden in the carpet. A mat also adds cushioning that can prevent damage to dropped beads and gemstones.

317. Find a container to meet your needs.

When storing your beading supplies, you will need several containers to hold various sizes and shapes of tools. These can be found in craft stores, sporting goods stores, or hardware stores. Fishing tackle boxes and containers intended for nuts and bolts work well for holding beads.

Craft Mates Lockables is a brand of plastic boxes that have individual compartments that can be opened one at a time. This type of container prevents major spills. These boxes can be stacked on a shelf or stored in a drawer. They are available online or in hobby and craft stores.

Sort all supplies by function. Put all tools together, and beads and stones together.

318. Hang beads on a string.

If you like to keep beads on the string they came on, put hooks or nails on the wall or in a Peg-Board or bulletin board and hang the strings from them. After using beads from a strand, knot the string and hang it back on the hook.

319. Keep beads sorted to maximize efficiency.

It may seem tedious to separate all of your beads by type and color, but it will save you so much time as you craft. Use a container with individual locking compartments so you only need to sort once.

If you have a lot of supplies in one color, consider using a separate storage container for each color. For example, store all red beads, stones, and matching thread in one container; all blue beads, stones and threads in another.

320. Organize yarn by category.

Gather every skein, ball, and loose pieces of yarn and sort them into separate piles by color, texture, weight (sport, baby, worsted, bulky, etc.) and type of fiber.

Store each category in lidded, clear plastic containers. If you have a lot of yarn to store, empty five-gallon plastic ice cream buckets make great containers. Label the containers with the amount of skeins and weight.

321. Storage ideas for straight knitting needles.

There are several ways to store straight needles:
- a decorative wine box
- long pencil cases (found in the art aisle of craft stores) labeled on the outside with the size of the needle
- an oatmeal box covered with decorative paper
- a cloth knitting needle roll (find them online or in select yarn shops, or make your own following tutorials and free patterns online)

322. Storage ideas for circular knitting needles.

There are several ways to store circular needles:
- a three-ring binder with clear plastic page protectors to easily slip circular needles in; can be stored standing up on a shelf (label the page protector with the size of the needles)
- a circular needle clutch (find them in select yarn shops or make your own following online tutorials)
- a no-sew holder that hangs from a hook on the wall using wooden spools from a craft store (find a free tutorial on how to make one online)

323. Storage ideas for crochet hooks.

Some storage ideas for crochet hooks include:

- a hard plastic pencil case that is labeled on the outside so you know what it contains
- a plastic pencil bag with a zipper

324. Storage ideas for patterns.

Patterns come in a wide variety of media. Here are ideas for organizing each:

Books: Designate a space on your bookshelf for all knitting books. You can arrange by type of pattern (sweaters, scarfs, socks, etc.).

Pattern pamphlets: Create a hanging folder in your file drawer and label the tabs for each type of pattern. Or use a three-ring binder labeled with the types of patterns stored in it.

Online: Create a bookmark folder specifically for patterns you find online. If you are worried the site might disappear, copy and paste the pattern to a text document saved on your computer. Or print a hard copy and store that as you would a pamphlet.

E-reading devices: Store patterns and instructions by transferring them to a PDF format and then transfer to an e-reader using computer software programs, such as CutePDF.com.

325. Storage ideas for fabric.

Store fabric away from sunlight, as exposure to sunlight fades colors and weakens the fabrics.

Store like colors and like materials (cotton, wool, silk, polyester) together either by stacking on a shelf or in a plastic container. It is not necessary to use the lid as lids can make it inconvenient to reach the fabric inside. Lidless containers also allow air to circulate, which is better for the fabric. Either recycle the lid or tuck it away in the storage room if you think you might use it another time.

326. Storing fabric on wood shelves.

There is a difference of opinion whether it is okay to store fabric against bare wood. One opinion is fabric should not be stored against unfinished wood because acids from the wood can discolor and weaken the fabric. Others say they have stored fabric on wood for over twenty years and the fabric is still just fine. If in doubt, treat the wood with a polyurethane finish or cover it with another fabric such as an old sheet.

327. Keep your cutting table clear.

If you are a quilter or sewer, keep your cutting table free of items that don't belong there. It may seem like a time-saver to pile fabric on it, but the time you save now will be lost when you have to clear the table to use it. Items that could be left on your cutting table are a rotary cutter, omnigrid ruler, and a pincushion. If your work table is too low, raise it by using inexpensive bed risers available in variety stores.

328. Storage idea for sewing projects.

Store quilting or sewing projects together in an unused pizza box. Buy these boxes new and unused from your local pizza shop. Pizza boxes stack nicely and have enough room to hold your fabric and pattern. Label the box with the contents. For a more attractive look, cover the boxes with fabric or decorative paper, or paint them.

329. Storage ideas for batting.

Quilt batting will take up as much space as it is allowed. Keep batting in its original package and store on a shelf. Roll or tightly fold partially used pieces and secure them with a length of selvage or other thin strip of fabric. Measure the piece and pin the measurements to the tightly rolled or folded batting. Store these pieces in a container on a shelf.

330. Storage ideas for decorative paper.

There are many ways to store card stock and decorative paper:
- stacked cubicles with slots 3" (8cm) deep (like office mailboxes or paper displays in scrapbooking stores), separated by color and design
- stacking storage boxes with snapping lids (many hold papers up to 12" × 12" [30cm × 30cm] in size)
- a mix-and-match modular cube system with removable shelving and drawers for versatility

- clear plastic paper holders that can be placed vertically on a shelf
- attractive cardboard boxes designed to hold 12" × 12" (30cm × 30cm) scrapbook paper

331. Create a portable scrapbooking station.

If you scrapbook at classes, friends' homes, or in different rooms in your home, create a traveling station for paper and other supplies. Options include:
- large flat cases with handles
- a rolling tote custom-made for scrapbook supplies
- a large tote bag

There are a variety of choices online or at craft stores.

332. Storage ideas for wood-mounted stamps.

Separate your stamps by category and choose a storage option that lets you keep the categories separate. Some storage ideas are:
- a rolling cart with plastic drawers
- boxes on a shelf
- a tool box or tackle box

333. Storage ideas for clear acrylic stamps.

Never store clear acrylic stamps in direct sunlight. Two storage options are:

- Use old CD cases with the center disc holder removed. (Each case will hold four to six stamps.)
- Put the stamps on a transparency sheet and slip the sheet into a sheet protector in a three-ring binder. Use dividers to separate each category. If you have a lot of stamps, this method can get heavy. In that case, use smaller binders for each individual category.

334. Storage ideas for stickers.

Sort stickers by type (letters, travel, holiday, children, etc.), and keep each category in a separate container so you can quickly find what you want. Some options for organizing and storing stickers include:

- manila or legal-size envelopes, clearly labeled
- clear plastic or colored envelopes that are closed with a clasp or string

Designate one place to keep your stickers. It could be a drawer, box, basket, or hanging file.

THIRTEEN

Storage Areas

335 Create storage spaces in plain sight.

336 Choose furniture with hidden storage options.

337 Try adjustable tables with shelves.

338 Use a bookcase as a substitute closet.

339 Get more uses out of an armoire.

340 Add a window seat.

341 A table skirt hides it all.

342 Store items in benches.

343 Use vintage suitcases as end tables.

344 Assign specific homes for everything you store.

345 Assign themes to your storage areas.

346 Store items where they are convenient and safe.

347 Protect against mold and pests.

348 Organize storage areas by department or zone.

349 Use shelves instead of stacks.

350 Choose heavy-duty containers.

351 Don't overload containers.

352 Use containers within containers.

353 Color-code your storage bins.

354 Use specialty containers for decorations.

355 Purge decorations at the end of the season.

356 Evaluate storage areas each year.

357 How to store items for grown children.

358 A storage shed can reap long-term benefits.

359 Storage ideas for sports equipment.

360 Make take-and-run equipment bags.

361 Make room for your car in your garage.

362 Mark off your parking spot.

363 Storage ideas for tools.

364 Storage ideas for gardening tools.

365 Storage ideas for patio furniture.

335. Create storage spaces in plain sight.

What can you do when you don't have an attic, basement, or room for storage shelves? Get creative! You can have functional storage areas in plain sight by selecting items that serve two purposes—their primary purpose (e.g., seating or table area) and their secondary purpose, which is storage.

336. Choose furniture with hidden storage options.

Look for furniture that has hidden storage and compartments. Choose a coffee table with shelves that are divided and can hold a basket in each compartment. Or use an old trunk as a coffee table. Use an ottoman with a lid that lifts off easily and has secret storage space inside. Purchase end tables with drawers or cabinets.

337. Try adjustable tables with shelves.

If you have a wide hallway, a drop-leaf table with a shelf underneath can hold baskets for extra storage. The surface can hold small things like keys, mail, and cell phone charger stations. The shelf below can hold larger lidded containers that can hold anything you need to store.

338. Use a bookcase as a substitute closet.

Another option for a wide hallway is adding a tall bookcase. Place baskets or cloth bins on the shelves and use them to store items you would keep in a hall closet or linen closet.

339. Get more uses out of an armoire.

In addition to extra storage space for clothing, armoires can be modified to be used as:

- linen storage
- mini-bar that stores wine glasses and drink accessories
- a home office—computer, printer, and stationery storage
- cleaning, laundry, and pet supply storage
- additional kitchen cabinet space
- craft supply cupboard

340. Add a window seat.

If you have the space, add a window seat in any room in your home. This is a great place to store seasonal pillows, bedding, quilts used as throws, or children's toys if it is not too deep.

341. A table skirt hides it all.

Attach a table skirt to a table using Velcro. Place baskets or bins underneath to store items, such as puzzles, games, free weights, magazines or books, linens, and even seldom used dishes and platters or small pieces of luggage.

342. Store items in benches.

Repurpose any bench with a lid to store things, such as books, magazines, gloves, hats, or place mats and napkins. Place a pillow made to fit on top and secure with ties. You don't need to own a piano to have a piano bench. Look for them at flea markets, thrift stores, and antique malls. Place the bench in a corner or against a wall for portable additional seating.

343. Use vintage suitcases as end tables.

Stack several vintage suitcases on top of each other and use them as an end table. Store anything inside that fits; extra glasses, dishes, seasonal clothes, guest linens, ribbon, fabric, and holiday decorations, to name a few. Store items here that aren't used on a frequent basis. For an artsy look, use Mod Podge to affix pictures on the outside and spray with polyurethane to protect.

344. Assign specific homes for everything you store.

Tossing things in a spare room, attic, or basement doesn't constitute storage. Identify everything you keep in your storage spaces and create specific homes for each item. Remember to keep like items together and use labeled containers. Label shelves so you know where to put things and find them when you want them.

Storage space is valuable, so create spaces that serve the purposes you need instead of using these areas as dumping grounds for items that don't have an identified place "to live" in your home.

345. Assign themes to your storage areas.

If you have multiple storage areas (garage, shed, storage room, or attic), keep like things together in one area so you don't have to search more than one place for things you need. For example, you could keep all sporting equipment in your garage, all old clothing in your attic, all bulk or extra food in your storage room.

346. Store items where they are convenient and safe.

When you decide where to keep things, consider the conditions and the accessibility in each area. Keep frequently used items in easy-to-access storage spaces. If your basement is damp or musty, be aware of potential issues with mold and odor. Keep objects sensitive to heat and cold out of attics, sheds, and garages.

347. Protect against mold and pests.

Consider including a packet of silica gel (a moisture absorber) in each container if you have problems with mold or moisture forming in the container. These can be purchased online or you can reuse the packets that come in new shoes, purses, coats, etc. Be sure to keep them out of reach of children. Keep clothes fresh and moth-free by packing dryer sheets or cedar chips in the container.

348. Organize storage areas by department or zone.

Make it easy to find what you are looking for and to put things away by organizing your storage areas by department or zone. Follow the department store model and assign shelves and corners to specific categories, such as holiday, clothing, tools, and children's items.

349. Use shelves instead of stacks.

Some containers will stack very well, but stacks don't allow for convenient access. You have to move all of the containers in the stack to reach the bottom one. Set up shelving whenever possible to use vertical space without stacking too high.

350. Choose heavy-duty containers.

All containers are not created equal. Use containers that are best suited for the climate you live in. Clear plastic containers can crack with use and in climates that go from extreme heat to extreme cold. Choose bins made of strong thick plastic or rubber. Also look for lids that fit snugly. Use containers of the same size so they stack easier and fit together without gaps of wasted space.

Always label every container with the contents. Don't write directly on the container as you may decide to move contents from one container to another container. Label options include:

- attaching a 3" × 5" (8cm × 13cm) note card with tape
- applying masking or painter's tape and writing on it
- a label maker

351. Don't overload containers.

You may be tempted to use as few containers as possible, but don't overload storage boxes and bins. Make sure they are easy to lift and move. Placing items so you can retrieve them when you need them is key to organized storage.

352. Use containers within containers.

Save shelf space by putting small containers in large bins. This protects small items and keeps them together while making for fewer items to move. Label the top of the small containers so they are easy to see as you go through the bin.

353. Color-code your storage bins.

A quick way to find your holiday decorations is to coordinate the color of the bins to each holiday, such as: blue for the Fourth of July, orange or black for Halloween, red or green for Christmas, etc. Use labels in addition to the color-coding system.

354. Use specialty containers for decorations.

Whenever possible, use containers designed to hold specific types of decorations (tree ornaments, wreaths, etc.). It makes it easy to store them quickly and safely. Shop after-holiday sales to buy containers at reduced prices.

Store decorations in your semi-storage area. This is the area where they can be easily accessed but aren't taking up valuable space within your home.

355. Purge decorations at the end of the season.

The best time to purge holiday decorations is when you're putting them out and putting them away.

Each season, as you get out holiday decorations, look at each decoration in every container. Fix those that are broken or throw them away. Only keep those you enjoy and bring you happy memories.

If you no longer want to use a decoration, give it to a family member if it is something they have wanted or donate it to your local thrift shop.

When you buy new holiday decorations, identify old decorations you can get rid of to keep your collection up-to-date and manageable.

356. Evaluate storage areas each year.

Evaluate what you are storing in each of your storage areas once a year. You'll remember what you have and get rid of what you don't need.

Look through each container within the storage area and evaluate each item. If you haven't used it in the past year, do you still need to keep it? Is it an item you could take out of storage and start using again? You don't need to check the long-term storage containers.

You can go through all your storage areas at once or break them up throughout the year so you evaluate a few each season. This is also a good time to evaluate your organizing system in the storage area and make changes if needed.

This may seem like a large task, but if you keep up with it every year, your storage area will stay organized and you'll have fewer items to look through as you cull the clutter each year.

357. How to store items for grown children.

If you have agreed to store your grown children's things, ask your children to go through their boxes and bins and purge as much as possible first so you will have as few things as possible to take up space in your home. After you have agreed to store their things until they have a home of their own or are out of college (or whenever), don't send them on a guilt trip about their storage. This just creates bad feelings.

Store their boxes and bins in your home in a place designated as long-term storage. These boxes don't need to be accessible because your children won't be going through them until they move them. Put these items on top shelves, either in a storage room or in a seldom used closet. If you have the space, store all of their items together.

358. A storage shed can reap long-term benefits.

If your grown children have more things than you can store in your home, consider buying a shed and placing it on your property. Unless you can effectively control the temperature in your shed, don't store valuables here if they are sensitive to heat and cold. When they take their boxes, you can repurpose the shed for a gardening shed or to store lawn and garden supplies or a playhouse for the grandkids. Your children can be responsible for the actual purchase of the shed by making payments to you. This is a win-win situation as their things will be accessible if they need them and it won't be wasted money spent on a storage unit somewhere else.

359. Storage ideas for sports equipment.

Keep all your sporting equipment together in one location so you can find it when you want it. The garage or a storage shed are most logical because equipment is used outside and is often dirty. The basement or patio is a third option if you don't have a garage or shed.

Use galvanized metal or heavy plastic garbage cans to store a variety of equipment, such as ski poles, baseball bats, and hockey sticks. Use separate cans for winter sports and summer sports. Toss balls in a small garbage can or in a mesh bag hanging on the wall. Use separate containers for each sport if needed.

Purchase wall-mounted racks for equipment, such as skis, snowboards, bikes or golf bags. Hang bikes from the ceiling using large "S" hooks. Hang a bike pump on the wall to inflate balls and bike tires.

360. Make take-and-run equipment bags.

If your children need to take equipment to practices, create take-and-run bags. In separate duffel bags for each sport, place all equipment needed for each sport. Hang these on separate hooks in the garage when not being used. Use a permanent marker to label each bag with the sport, the child's name, and the contents.

361. Make room for your car in your garage.

The garage is meant primarily to house your car. Everything else in the garage is probably worth a lot less, so organize this space

so your car fits in its "home." Follow these steps to make room
for your car:

1. Take everything out—yes, everything. Donate, toss, or
   sell items you never use.
2. Pull your car in the garage and mark off how much space
   it takes up, including when you open the doors. Leave
   this area open when you return items to the garage.
3. Group like items together when putting them back.
4. Divide the space in your garage into different storage
   zones for all things stored here.
5. Attach shelves or cabinets to the walls or set up free-
   standing, heavy-duty metal shelves for storage.
6. Find new homes for items that no longer fit—or continue
   purging. This will be easier if you've already organized
   your other storage areas.

362. Mark off your parking spot.

Avoid pulling your car in too far or not far enough by hanging
a tennis ball or rubber ball on a string from the ceiling so it just
touches your windshield when you reach the appropriate spot.
This is especially helpful for beginner drivers.

363. Storage ideas for tools.

Use a Peg-Board or a wall-mounted tool rack to store larger
tools (power drill, hand saws, levels, etc.). Use sturdy storage
bins with drawers to store nails, screws, wire, putty knives, and

other small tools. Label each drawer. Use a metal or heavy-plastic toolbox to corral basic tools, such as screwdrivers, hammer, pliers, utility knife, safety glasses, tape measure, and gloves. A toolbox helps keep tools clean and dry and there is an assigned place to put them after use. It also makes the tools mobile so you can use them around the house and then easily return them to the right place.

364. Storage ideas for gardening tools.

Designate an area specifically for garden tools so they will be handy to reach when you want them. Depending on the type of space you have available, you could keep them in your garage, shed, or basement. Select one location for all of them.

- Use nails or install metal brackets or racks on the walls to hang long-handled tools.
- Install a Peg-Board to hold a variety of tools. Draw an outline around each tool with a marker to identify where to hang it after using it.
- Use plastic, wood, or metal free-standing containers with drawers for small tools, such as trowels, sprinkler nozzle, twine, gloves, and scissors.
- Install a wall hanger for you garden hose for winter storage.
- Keep tools sharp by removing dirt after each use. Use a three-in-one light-machine oil to wipe down the metal parts.
- Store fertilizer and potting soil in a covered container.

365. Storage ideas for patio furniture.

Winter weather is hard on patio furniture and properly storing it during the off season will greatly extend its life. It's time to store patio furniture when it's too cold to sit outside and enjoy the night air.

Before you store the furniture, thoroughly clean each piece using a soft cloth or sponge and your favorite all-purpose cleaner. Let it dry completely. Consider painting pieces that are starting to rust to prevent the rust from spreading.

Take off the cushions and pillows and store them in a shed or garage to keep them dry.

Stack lightweight chairs together to maximize space. Store in a shed or garage if space permits. Or store outside under or on top of or next to tables. Secure a tarp around all the furniture, tying tightly to keep it from blowing off in heavy winds. Or invest in heavy-duty outdoor furniture covers.

Conclusion

Organizing is an on-going process. Life happens and circumstances change, so you will need to continually evaluate the organizing systems in your home.

If you struggle to stay organized, work on applying the concepts in this book on a daily, weekly, or monthly basis. If you create new habits, being organized will become a way of life.

Even with strong organizing habits in place, there will be times when your organizing systems no longer work for you. This typically happens after a change or during transition. Maybe you remodeled or moved someone into or out of your home. Or maybe you've just accumulated too much stuff and it's time to purge the old. When your systems fail and you feel disorganized, identify what the problem is and use the tips in this book to find new solutions that work for you.

I find great joy and satisfaction being invited into women's homes to help them organize and get rid of clutter. I have seen lives changed as they make room for what they truly love so they can enjoy things that "light them up," bring them peace, and save them money and time. My hope is this book will help you create a home you truly enjoy.

Index

About the Author

Marilyn Bohn is an organizing expert and author of *Go Organize! Conquer Clutter in 3 Simple Steps* (Betterway Home). She is also the founder of Get It Together Organizing. She has been featured on KSL, KUTV-TV, KJZZ-TV, KSL Newsradio, and KLBC Radio, and has taught multiple organizing classes within her community. Her articles have appeared in local and national newspapers and company newsletters. Marilyn's focus is to help people reduce clutter in their homes, offices, and lives. In addition to face-to-face organizing assistance, Marilyn also offers convenient virtual online organizing via her website, www.marilynbohn.com.

Before becoming a professional organizer, she worked in the social service field as a child protection worker and a contract analyst. She is a member of the National Association of Professional Organizers.

Acknowledgments

A special thank you to my girls, who thought this was a terrific idea for a book and believed in me and encouraged me as I wrote.

Thank you to my friends, who were excited about this book and would check in often to see how I was doing.

Thanks also to Jackie, my editor at Betterway Home, who was always positive and encouraging with every chapter I submitted.

Dedication

To the amazing women in my life who have guided and inspired me:
My mother, Margaret; Zola and Emma, my aunts; my daughters, Cindy, Pamela, Debbie, Julie, and Janice; and my cousin, Kay.

Published by Betterway Home, an imprint of F+W Media, Inc., 10151 Carver Road, Suite 200, Blue Ash, Ohio, 45242. (800) 289-0963. First Edition.

Other fine Betterway Home books are available from your local bookstore and online suppliers. Visit our website at www.betterwaybooks.com.

16   15   14   13   12   5   4   3   2   1

ISBN 978-1-4403-1841-2

Distributed in Canada by Fraser Direct
100 Armstrong Avenue, Georgetown, Ontario, Canada L7G 5S4
Tel: (905) 877-4411

Distributed in the U.K. and Europe by F&W Media International, LTD
Brunel House, Newton Abbot, Forde Close, TQ12 4PU, UK
Tel: (+44) 1626 323200, Fax: (+44) 1626 323319
E-mail: enquiries@fwmedia.com

Distributed in Australia by Capricorn Link
P.O. Box 704, S. Windsor NSW, 2756 Australia
Tel: (02) 4577-3555

Edited by Jacqueline Musser
Designed by Clare Finney
Production Coordinated by Mark Griffin